KIT & COMMUNITY

KIT & COMMUNITY

Football's Shirt Stories

Matt Riley

First published by Pitch Publishing, 2024

Pitch Publishing
9 Donnington Park,
85 Birdham Road,
Chichester,
West Sussex,
PO20 7AJ
www.pitchpublishing.co.uk
info@pitchpublishing.co.uk

A CIP catalogue record is available for this book
from the British Library.

ISBN 978-1 80150 735 6

Typesetting and origination by Pitch Publishing

Printed and bound in Great Britain by TJ Books Limited, Padstow, Cornwall

Contents

For Karen. Nothing else matters.

Acknowledgements

SO MANY shirt stories have melted my heart and emptied my bank account through a buying frenzy after hearing tales told by passionate, committed and creative people. I am more convinced than ever about a shirt's power to share values and drive creativity, kindness and collegiality. I (try to) teach my students that opinions can be tossed around without thought or awareness of consequences and attitudes can be shonky and half-baked, but our values speak to the core of who we are. Shirts are the calling card for those heartfelt foundations that underpin our character.

To Kieran Maguire, 'the Count of Companies House', who shares the passion with partner in podcast crime Kevin Day, thank you for your support of both books (especially for sneakily displaying *Kit and Caboodle* on your *BBC Breakfast* interview bookshelf, Kieran) and the inspiring foreword you're about to read. To their producer, Guy Kilty, thanks so much for the content about their stunning football shirts that go to support our friends at Gambling With Lives. Paul Watson, your book *Up Pohnpei* was truly inspirational. John Nicholson, a man whose bold, timely and often eviscerating writing I have long read and admired, I appreciate you agreeing to write a chapter. Even more than *Kit and Caboodle*, writing this book helped me meet and listen to some amazing people like Gig and Rog Stansfield. Thanks for sharing the heartbreaking but inspiring story of your son Adam's untimely death and the power his shirts have to drive the great work you do for the Adam Stansfield Foundation.

To Mental Health Football, Adam from Mind, Body & Sole, and Hull City Supporters' Trust director and former chairman Geoff Bielby for showing the beautiful game's power catalysed through a stunning kit that promotes support, friendship and a haven in a difficult world.

The fantastic cross-stitch shirt designs by Dave Murray that watch over me as I type this show just how much innovation and creativity there is out there in the football shirt community. Dan at Rock 'n' Roll Football Shirts fought through the tough Covid lockdown times to keep his dream alive of high quality music and football crossover shirts, and Steve Wyatt from the mighty Dilton Marsh Wanderers shows how pushing the design dial right up to 11 can have some surprising and heartwarming consequences. For probably the most 'out-there' kit in my collection, thanks to Evan Jackson for telling us more about a truly bonkers and brilliant creation for American club Sporting Waterloo FC and the ever-inspiring Icarus. To the king of concept kits, Sithuralom, thanks so much for sharing your superb Nascar templates. Talking of our friends across the pond, it was fantastic to connect with Proud Owls, the independent group of LGBTQIA+ and allied supporters of Union Omaha.

Talking of cool creativity, I appreciate Matt and his design team at Kit and Bone's help and creative input. 'Dull is Dead' according to the company's slogan. It certainly is. Another eye-catching image was the beautiful black and gold creation of Loch Ness FC shared by its designer Martin Mainland – a shirt that looked elegant and helped raise money for local causes. This was an approach shared by fellow Scottish team Nairn County. Thanks to Michael Bochel for telling the deeply moving story behind their charity kit design. To Christopher Payne for walking me through the stunning design decisions for the achingly elegant York City centenary shirt – thank you so much for an inspirational story that speaks to the history of the city and club, celebrating both with a stunning chocolate confection. To the legends that are Tanya and Jayme from Football Shirts For Charity, it was great to meet you and witness your fierce determination to use shirts for the greater good. Talking of which, the incredible work done by Grassroot Soccer as their senior manager, marketing and communications officer Ethan McCoy shared with me in early 2023 was catalysed through one of my favourite shirt designs.

So, as a great man once said, 'But hey, enough of my yakking.' Welcome to *Kit and Community*.

Foreword by Kieran Maguire

AS A schoolboy, going to the local sports shop and staring enviously at the football shirts with the 'official' badges and manufacturer logos was a weekly ritual. I can still remember looking at the first Admiral catalogue and having my first football shirt World Cup competition, assiduously spending hours writing out the kits on to pieces of paper, and drawing them out against each other in a knockout before deciding on the ultimate winner (Manchester United away with the three stripes narrowly defeating the Wales yellow change strip if anyone cares).

Football kits are incredible in that they turn fans (usually middle-aged or older men) from people who have no colour or style coordination into the full Trinny and Susannah for 24 hours two or three times a year. Width of stripes, collars or no collars, shades or red/blue/green etc. become absolutely critical, and regardless of the final conclusion on the latest offerings from the club, will still be bought, usually in one size too small on the grounds that the diet is going to start 'soon'.

Football is all about shared memories, shared experiences, misery as well as joy, and that is why kits matter too. Many footballers are superstitious, fans too. Some kits are deemed to be 'lucky', until the team loses in them; some are the opposite, so finding out what kit is being worn at away matches can take on great importance in the pub on the day the game takes place. Memories of 'that' match where 'that' player scored 'that' goal are framed by the kit that was worn on the day.

As a Brighton fan, my most expensive piece of football memorabilia is the shirt worn by loanee Paul McShane, who scored the winning goal with a flying header, which upon closer inspection turned out to be a flying shoulder, against rivals Crystal Palace at Selhurst Park in 2005. Brighton at the time were playing at a converted athletics stadium, and were both skint in terms of finances, as well as sponsored by the record label Skint too.

However, Crystal Palace's red-and-blue-striped kit was deemed to clash with Brighton's home kit (blue and white stripes), away kit (red) and third kit (blue). Therefore a special one-off white kit was worn on the day, and the club auctioned off all the shirts following the match in a bid to generate much-needed cash. The shirt was signed, framed and took pride of place at home, generating confused looks from guests wondering why anyone in command of their faculties would pay £835 for a shirt worn by someone few have ever heard of.

The shirt, however, proved to be a curse for whoever was its subsequent owner. I was soon divorced and living without a proper home, so it was auctioned again (for charity) and the lucky recipient themselves also ended up divorced within two years and so sold it back to me.

Matt's original *Kit and Caboodle* is a labour of love, a true coffee table book in that you can look at individual sections and see the enthusiasm and dedication that has gone into researching the contents. The stories behind the kits, why they matter, the history of the badge, the importance of the crest to the town or city which they represent, embody the good that football can bring. In what is an increasingly fractured world, the shirt is a symbol of unity, hope and love for where you were born, brought up, fell in love or the many reasons why football continues to be the most important of the unimportant things in life.

This follow-up book takes things further, and rightly so. Like many football fans, I want to be buried in the shirt of the team I love (not the McShane one, it's too unlucky) and Matt's book explains why that love is supreme, and why it matters. Read it, turn the pages lovingly, smile and occasionally wipe a tear from your eye. This book encapsulates the game and the importance of the fan, its biggest investor.

1

John Nicholson

I'VE ALWAYS admired John Nicholson's work (and our similar taste in heavy metal music) as a prodigious writer of 18 novels and five football-focussed books, all of which I have devoured. In 2010, *We Ate All the Pies* was long-listed for the William Hill Sports Book of the Year award, halfway through his two decades as one of Football365's most high-profile writers. It was an honour to share *Kit and Caboodle* with him. It was an even bigger honour that he agreed to write for this book.

Here is a short review by me of *Can We Have Our Football Back Yet?*, his 2021 release, to illustrate just why *Kit and Community*, which gives a stage to values-driven people, is the perfect fit with John.

John's writing is a barnstorming, eviscerating and much-needed antidote to asinine back-channelling by nation states preparing the ground for the next iteration of the European Franchise League. *Can We Have Our Football Back Yet?* makes us fall in love with the Luddites.

This book aims its prodigious fire on 'the Premier League mindwipe propaganda' that fuels heartless manipulators intent on bleeding yet another revenue stream for their hollow aggrandisement. The Premier League universe perpetuates 'some sort of demented pit of weirdness, where normal moralities and mores are not in play'. Gloriously obliterating television rights set up to artificially pump Premier League stock and dump on fans as it sets sail for new global markets to exploit, John stands up for the fan who only wants to feel fleeting moments of joy that a game at 'Cappielow in the pouring rain' can provide just as easily as Old Trafford.

This is a book that gives us pause to think as we are ushered into football as another opportunity to free us from our money. Never knowingly under-told, his tales come from the heart of a man we can trust with the beacon of bloody-minded and righteous indignation.

Thank you, John, and over to you:

'If you're under the age of 45 you won't remember that football shirts didn't have advertising on them until the late 1970s and early 80s. Strips did change from time to time, but there was no such thing as a shirt sponsor, a shirt sleeve sponsor, a training top sponsor or indeed any sponsor at all. Clubs were largely funded by in-ground advertising, 80 per cent of home gate ticket sales and 20 per cent of the gate for away games. They didn't need to get in bed with gambling companies and bloody autocratic states. A better world? It is hard to argue otherwise if you have any sort of functioning moral compass. But for those under 45 I can see how odd it must seem to think of a blank shirt, free of brand endorsement. Fifty years is a long time, long enough for there to be nostalgia, not about having no sponsors, but about specific eras of sponsorship, be it the Manchester United "Sharp" shirt or the Liverpool "Hitachi" top.

'Liverpool were the first professional English club to have a shirt sponsor when they took Hitachi's money, though Hibernian had beaten them to it with their Bukta deal in 1977. What is often forgotten all these years later, now that shirt sponsorship is all-encompassing and omnipresent, is that the concept of putting advertising on football shirts was very, very controversial. Anecdotally, I would say the vast majority of fans were against it. At my club, Middlesbrough FC, a common view was that putting a sponsor name and logo on the shirt would be a very bad thing. The shirt was the club's emblem and should not be for sale to the highest bidder. Shirts, in some way, were seen as sacred and should be above and beyond being mere advertising hoardings. Adverts would defile them. The good name of the club would be exploited by the advertiser. We would become associated with something we wouldn't want to be associated with.

'Today, such concerns, such morals, whether at the Boro or anywhere else, simply don't exist and the football shirt real estate has been sold off in its entirety to that most weaselly of expressions, "official partners". The argument then and now was that it'd help the club finances and thus help the team win more games. Oddly enough, relegated clubs also have sponsors, so that was always a lie. This is all part of the broader culture of the monetisation of football. The endless quest to increase income in order to be able to pay more for players and pay the players more, all in pursuit of greater success, whatever that rather nebulous concept might mean. However, this was always destined to be a road that would lead the game down an ever more destructive spiral. This pursuit of ever greater income in order to compete was always just going to increase inflation, which in turn would mean clubs would need more money and have to sell off more acreage of space on shirts, in the ground and via deals with pot noodle partners and incontinence bag suppliers for ever greater amounts of money to ever less effect.

'Across 50 years, the need for cash went up and up and up. What started out as fairly humble sponsors like, in Middlesbrough's case, Heritage Hampers, has now been taken over by airlines from oppressive autocracies and gambling companies that specialise in exploiting the vulnerable. There seems little or no moral judgement, though at last some are a bit queasy about promoting gambling. Usually, the one offering the most cash wins. At the top of the pyramid, ironically, those shirt sponsors for betting companies don't even drum up much cash. Across the 20 clubs in the Premier League, total income from shirt sponsors is around £70m per year, or an average of about £3.5m per club. That'd pay David de Gea's wages for just ten weeks. But the advertising culture is now endemic and is something that must be exploited even though it doesn't bring in enough money to make a significant difference to finances.

'With multi-billion-dollar dollar oil states now owning clubs, pumping hundreds of millions of pounds into the club, why do they even bother with a sponsor paying maybe ten million quid over three years? The answer is they're not. Or at least, it's changing. For example Newcastle United, owned by Saudi Arabia's Public Investment Fund, will be sponsored by Saudia, Saudi Arabia's national airline. And the fee for the sponsorship will be, just as it was at Manchester City, far higher than the market would normally demand, but will satisfy the Premier League's Profit and Sustainability rules, allowing them to spend more on players. Be in no doubt, the fix is in. And if anything is done about it, which is unlikely because it devalues the Premier League brand and the Premier League doesn't want that, it'll be a long way in the future and little more than a slap on the wrist. That is the new value of advertisers.

'The lack of protest among football fans about this state of affairs suggests how complete the brainwashing has been. Alongside this growth of sponsorship has come a massive growth in "official merchandise". As you will remember if you're old enough, there was no such thing as official merchandise in the 1970s or before. If your club played in a blue shirt and blue shorts, you bought generic sports clothing off a local market stall or sports shop in those colours and you just said it was Chelsea or Southend, or whoever. It is worth saying that no one was unhappy with this state of affairs and it is clearly a more practical way of living. Every parent knows the pressure from kids to have the latest shirt. And there's always a new shirt. You can wear a heritage shirt with a 1990s sponsor on, but God forbid you wear last season's version. That was so last year. The ever-changing world of football shirts has created an insatiable demand, even going so far as to suggest that if you don't have the official strip then you're not a real fan. Buy the knock-off stuff and you don't love the club because you're depriving it of income.

'This is naked capitalism at its worst and it has made no one's life any better. And even more ironically, that claim isn't true because the club almost certainly will not benefit from you buying a shirt because it will have just been paid a flat fee by a company who will manufacture and supply them into shops. So by the time you go in to buy one, the club has already had as much money as it is going to get and the profit from the sale will go into the contract-holder's account, not the club's.

'I grew up wearing a red shirt with a white band across the centre, which I said was a Boro shirt and so it was a Boro shirt. No one questioned it. No one said it was inferior in any way. I also had a tangerine one with white crew-neck collar and cuffs which my mother had bought because she thought the colour would suit me. I said that was a Blackpool shirt. I didn't support Blackpool but that didn't matter. It was a football shirt and that's all there was to it. Again, no one said it wasn't a Blackpool shirt. No one cared. However, try passing this trick off on a fan these days and they will likely look at you with scorn. They want the official new strip from the club shop, usually at an exorbitant cost, often made by exploited developing world labour. How lovely. There seems to be absolutely no discomfort about the brands they de facto endorse by wearing those shirts. It doesn't even seem to cross anyone's mind.

'To illustrate this blindness, I was once talking to a Newcastle fan a few years ago when their new sponsor was Fun88. I made a joke about the poor quality of football not being much fun. He didn't get the joke. When I explained, it was clear he didn't really see Fun88 at all. All he saw was the black and white stripes. It was as though those letters were just part of the pattern. I found that most odd indeed. He certainly didn't care that his club was sponsored by an online casino and sportsbook. It's a massive con job, of course. For all clubs like to pretend otherwise, there is nothing special about official merchandise. Quite the opposite. Some come with a tamper-proof seal of approval to ensure you're buying a genuine shirt. Those tags are, of course, bootlegged, as are the shirts themselves, often by the very same factories making the official shirts. It's all such a racket; an industry full of scoundrels. I've seen fake England shirts and genuine shirts and there was no difference between them at all except one cost £25 and one £60. The human rights of those making either seemed of little genuine concern.

'But it didn't stop at replica shirts. Club crests which had long adorned a team's shirts became another thing to exploit. Most top clubs have changed their badges to make them able to trademark them and prosecute anyone using it. It wouldn't surprise me if the cost of lawyers to police the global market for bootleg badges and bootleg shirts costs the club more than any money they may have lost by them being bootlegged in the first place.

'Back in the day, no one would ever have thought of trademarking a badge, so much so that you could buy packets of club badges from sports shops to sew on to the shirt you got off the market. Sometimes the badges were heraldic-style reproductions of the town's civic crest and as such communally owned by everyone who lived there. How different from today where badges were redesigned to be unique enough to be trademarked. The economics of the football shirt, from those unbranded days to the contemporary exploitation of every square inch in pursuit of ever great levels of income, is a journey that mirrors the development of football from a working-class game, played by the people for the people, into corporate global capitalism's favourite wet dream, into the plaything of billionaires, to the favoured way to whitewash your country's appalling human rights record.

'It all goes to show that marketing can overcome logical thought. Personally, I could never understand why anyone would want to wear a T-shirt with SuperDry on. I mean, why would you? What do the words even mean in this context? But millions do. I don't know what they get out of it. Remember those big DKNY T-shirts with a black letters on a white shirt? They were popular in the 1990s. They were so easy to copy and print on to a better quality shirt and sell for half the price. I knew people in Manchester who had a factory doing exactly that with DKNY and other "designer" brands. They were sold to people as the real thing, only at 30 per cent of the price. Punters were happy with their purchase until they learned it wasn't the real thing, then they were disgruntled. That is the perfect illustration of the official/unofficial existential conundrum that football has so successfully exploited.

'Of course, not everyone has fallen for it. The replica shirt trade supplies the market with copies of the brandless shirts of the 1970s to those who, like me, are squeamish about the modern-day exploitative versions. The branded shirts of the late 70s and early 80s were the canaries in the coal mine. They were the thin end of a wedge so big that it has pulled international politics and human rights organisations into its orbit. This was achieved because shirts are important to fans. They're a badge of identity and a bookmark in your life's timeline. And after all, players, managers and owners come and go, but only the fans remain, so what are we cheering on really? The name above the door and the shirt, that's what. It is the only material thing in our relationship with football clubs, that's why they are so important and that's why they have been so successfully exploited for profit.

'It is hard to see this as progress but because the "official" shirt mindwipe has been so effective across the best part of two generations, there's no going back to the simple days of unadorned unofficial shirts any more. Capitalism has won both the battle and the war.'

2

Stanno's Shirt

'Sing a song for Stanno.
We will never let you go.
You'll always be.
At City with me.'

WHEN ADAM Stansfield arrived at Exeter City in 2006 after spells with Yeovil Town and Hereford United, very few fans realised the seismic effect his four-year spell would have on our team's fortunes and how his footballing DNA would course through our club for decades to come. He was our very own Steve Bull (one for the kids there) in attitude and hairstyle. Both men gave every ounce of energy for every minute of every game for the shirt. Not in some vacuous crest-kissing way for monetised social media, but drawing on determination underscored by battering, battling skill. Stanno's footballing passion was passed down from his dad Roger, a huge Nottingham Forest fan. Roger's description of his son as someone who 'just kept plugging away' was one of the many reasons why

the Big Bank took him into our hearts and never let him go.

Adam didn't even turn professional until he was 23, by which age Bull had been playing for Wolverhampton Wanderers for a couple of years in the Fourth Division against Exeter before going up as champions in 1988. Adam would go on to grace the City shirt for four years, playing 142 times and scoring 37, often barnstorming, goals. He joined us while we were in the Conference and was in the team that won a return to the Football League after beating Cambridge United 1-0 at Wembley in the 2008 play-off final. But, in April 2010, he would be diagnosed with colorectal cancer. Then, despite surgery and chemotherapy, he died four months later at the heartbreakingly young age of 31.

Fast forward to 2 September 2022, and the bipolar platform of Twitter was lurching from City desperately needing new blood to what seemed like delusional fantasist talk of Adam's son Jay choosing to leave Premier League Fulham for our little trust-run club in sleepy Devon. Claim and counter-claim ricocheted around this often fact-free environment and, by the evening, there were even those wearied by the talk of Stanno 2.0 joining us. We are so conditioned to players, once in the hermetically sealed Premier League universe, preferring to warm subs' benches rather than leave for the Championship or, heaven forbid, League One. Stockpiled talent carelessly collected by state-owned behemoths kick their heels and kill careers while collecting outrageously expensive tat for Instagram to gorge on. But then, at 4.51pm, the club sent out a 'nine-minute warning tweet' teasing a new player we all knew could only be Our Boy. The video showed the shirt (which had been retired by the club after Adam's death), the number nine and a dozen years of chanting for Stanno melded into one pure moment of joy. Like a street-corner born-again Christian, seeing that shirt I knew it was him. I had to tell someone, anyone. 'Have you accepted Stanno into your life? I know you are only here to deliver the post, but this was Stanno's will.'

Every week as I stood on the Big Bank basking in the sunshine or stamping my frozen feet, we sang our ode to Stanno. When the Adam Stansfield Stand (financed by the sale of Ollie Watkins to Brentford) was still under construction, the house-sized Stanno shirt would often be hoisted across the emerging structure that also followed us to our three heartbreaking visits to Wembley play-off disaster (at least only our cardboard cut-out selves were there to witness the hat-trick of heartbreak). When it was placed over us on the Big Bank, there was something collegially spiritual about reaching up to touch his shirt together and move it on for other fans to commune with. There always seemed to be onions sliced in the pie shop to our left on days when that happened. Strange.

That number nine shirt teased on a Friday evening by our amazing media team of Craig and Scott had been retired for nine years. Suddenly we knew. No one else would wear it other than Jay, who had left us in 2020 to join Fulham where he made four appearances, was capped for England's under-18 and under-19 teams and, displaying his dad's Steve Bull-style shaven head and furious tenacity that drew Stanno to our hearts, now one of our own was coming home (admittedly on loan) after maturing through our academy system.

When Adam's parents spoke to The Athletic's Peter Rutzler in January 2022, the inspiring memories their son forged wearing the City red and white allowed them to cope with his death by creating the Adam Stansfield Foundation to help save the lives of others. As well as educating people on the insidious signs of bowel cancer,

it also makes magic happen by focussing on one simple mission statement that changes lives for the better. As it declares on its website, 'The foundation is committed to providing charitable funds for young people/youth football teams who would benefit from the assistance.'

Underscoring this understated declaration comes a legion of stories. Young players who can't afford transport for training or trials. Those who love to play but wear glasses and need them protected with expensive covers. Children who can't afford boots. All of them are referred to the foundation for assistance and every act of support becomes a hat tip to the memory of Adam. When he passed, the family was inundated with previously unreported stories of his kindness, but it was the shirts filling up their postman's sack that gave those memories a place to breathe. As his mum Gig shared with Rutzler:

'At the Cat and Fiddle, Gig has a brought bag of vintage Exeter shirts to be passed on, ready for auction. From signed shirts to jockey breeches, all kinds of equipment have been sent their way. "The poor postman," says Jack [Vickery, who is a key driver of new income through tireless fundraising]. "The stuff just piles through the letterbox."

'"I suppose in a way, for us to be doing this foundation, it's always there. They have seen that their dad played a lot, they have all got their phones and see social media. But the ongoing stuff with Adam, with the foundation, you are conscious of it, it's almost like he's still with us."'

Iconic former Sky Sports presenter Jeff Stelling, who in 2017 used Exeter's St James Park to start his March for Men to raise money and awareness about prostate cancer by walking 15 marathons in 15 days and visiting 40 football clubs before finishing at the other St James' Park in Newcastle, spoke for us all on 3 September 2022: 'So today, assuming he [Jay] starts, he will run out for the club his dad graced, he'll play in the shadow of the stand named after his dad and he will wear the number nine shirt that had been retired: the shirt that his dad graced.'

Stanno's oversized shirt and his name that many of us carry on the back of our replica kits have sustained us for these dozen years. So many players have come and gone, often without leaving much of a mark apart from creating obsolescence for their shirts (I always used to chuckle seeing shirts from 2016 with former Spurs reserve Troy Archibald-Henville on the back. A man who was to make 20 appearances for the club – over four years). More than most clubs, the cream is often removed either before we have had a chance to enjoy it (Alfie Pond to Wolves and Ben Chrisene to Aston Villa being dispiriting examples) or made us dream of promotion before being picked up by lowballing Premier League clubs such as Ethan Ampadu to Chelsea, or respectful ones willing to pay a fair price with empowering add-ons as with Ollie Watkins to Brentford, but Stanno stands for stability. Despite leaving us in the worst way imaginable, our shirts carry the memories, aspirations and stories of a man who, like 'Bully', were of his place and never lost the feeling of wearing a shirt that gave him an invitation to enjoy what he loved more than anything. To play his beautiful game.

For visitors to City's Cliff Hill training ground (lovingly called by old codgers like me the Cat and Fiddle), there is a constant reminder of Stanno. Draped over a tailor's dummy is a classic red-and-white-striped home shirt of his above a pair of boots and team sheets, a matchday programme and also shirts from Stanno's two other clubs, Yeovil and Hereford. Part commemoration, part inspiration, these artefacts speak to a man steeped in the club and whose spirit continues to watch over every young hopeful or grizzled old-timer passing through the training ground gates. Jay also has his dad's shirts on the wall of his hallway alongside his own at home in London.

In late 2022 I spoke to Stanno senior's infectiously enthusiastic parents Gig and Roger (known as 'Rog'). I had ordered some foundation merchandise and, in a mark of their character, they came to my house to deliver it. You don't get that with Jeff Bezos. They told me more about what their number nine means to them, 'Right back to the beginning when Adam was born in the ninth month, we lived at 9 Exeter Street, Launceston (he was born in Plymouth hospital as that was nearest), so Devonian, not Cornish! So, there was a number nine and the Exeter path already starting. There were only a few times from getting his first nine shirt at the age of nine that he didn't have nine on his back. So when he signed for Exeter and was given the nine shirt it meant so much to him. He was very proud to be Exeter's number nine. It just seems so right to see "Stansfield 9". Adam's three sons – Jay, Taylor and Cody – have all worn nine for Twyford Spartans. So now for Jay to be at Exeter wearing that same shirt with such pride but in his own right, well that written path continues.

'After Adam passed, we thought the foundation we started in his name would last for about six months until we had donated all the money raised immediately after his funeral, but here we are 12 years later and it is bigger than ever. This is down to Adam's fans who proudly and emotionally display the giant "Stansfield 9" shirt and sing his song at every game. Not only are they paying a great tribute to Adam but they are keeping his name alive, so the charity thrives. There are so many young people who we help in grassroots football who weren't even born when Adam was playing, but they know who he is!

'Jay will wear that number nine shirt with the same pride as his dad and also with the same desire to give his all and do his very best for his team. And we continue to drive our car with reg number EX09TER now with a current "Stansfield 9" playing for Exeter.'

But then, in a heartbeat, it was 7 May 2023; the last time we would see Jay wear the red and white at St James Park. The Big Bank faithful trooped into SJP bluffly diffusing the emotion to come by distractions about the season behind us and what we had in store next time around, but we all knew there was bottlenecked emotion in need of cathartic release. This is not a sentence you usually write for a home game against Morecambe. Two hours later, Jay had scored a magnificent hat-trick (unfortunately at the away end) and ran to his dad's stand to pay homage to him and be engulfed by his team-mates. On that day, somewhere in Gloucestershire, a Sprocker puppy was being born. After two dogless decades, we went to see him and instantly fell in love. So now, ladies and gentlemen, welcome to our Stanno.

You'll always be at City with me.

* * *

Adam Stansfield Foundation: making a difference in the community

The Adam Stansfield Foundation, a UK-registered charity, continues to make a significant impact on the

lives of children and young people in Devon, Somerset, and Herefordshire. Established in 2011, the foundation's mission is twofold: to provide opportunities for young people to engage in football and to raise awareness of bowel cancer. Underpinning its mission, the Adam Stansfield Foundation has funded various projects, bringing football and hope to communities while championing the fight against bowel cancer. Let's take a closer look at some of the remarkable initiatives the foundation has supported over the years.

The Adam Stansfield Community Hub

Recognising the importance of dedicated spaces for local football clubs and community groups, the foundation established the Adam Stansfield Community Hub in Exeter. This state-of-the-art facility not only serves as a training ground but also features a welcoming cafe and versatile meeting spaces. The community hub has become a vibrant centre for fostering community spirit, allowing people to come together and celebrate the beautiful game. It provides a space where people can connect, share their passion for football, and create lasting memories.

The Adam Stansfield Bowel Cancer Research Fund

The foundation understands the significance of research in the fight against bowel cancer. To contribute to advancements in the diagnosis and treatment of this disease, it has established the Adam Stansfield Bowel Cancer Research Fund. This fund has been instrumental in supporting numerous research projects, including a groundbreaking study on the implementation of artificial intelligence to detect bowel cancer. By investing in research, the foundation aims to make a lasting impact in combating bowel cancer and improving the lives of those affected by it.

Impact and achievements

Since its inception, the Adam Stansfield Foundation has raised an incredible £150,000 through the support of generous donors and dedicated individuals. This reflects the unwavering commitment of the foundation's supporters to improving the lives of children and young people while raising awareness of bowel cancer. The funds raised have been instrumental in funding various projects, creating a tangible difference in the community. Through its initiatives, the foundation is fostering hope, resilience, and a sense of belonging among the young people it serves.

How to support the foundation

If you would like to join the Adam Stansfield Foundation in its mission to make a difference in the community, there are several ways to do so. One is to donate online at www.adamstansfieldfoundation. com. Every contribution, no matter the size, helps the team continue their vital work. Additionally, you can reach out to the foundation by calling 01392 423900 to learn about volunteering opportunities or to explore other ways to get involved. Together, we can support the foundation's efforts to create a brighter future for children and young people.

3

Honey, I Shrunk the Kits

STEPHEN FROM Tiny Jerseys tells the story of how he started making miniature versions of football's most iconic shirts, 'I think a lot of the folks I have met through the kit community are often surprised to learn that I'm American. As a large contingent of my online followers tend to be based in the UK, it's often assumed I am as well and for the most part it's generally unimportant, other than the sometimes-added complications and expense of shipping small clay statuettes from the US to the UK and elsewhere. I mention that I am American with no nefarious agenda other than to help put into context my relationship with soccer and to let those of you reading this chapter know that it will indeed be littered with reference to "soccer" and not "football" and "jerseys" instead of "kits".

'I would not be able to tell you now the name of most of the soccer teams I played on growing up (I know there was a "United" in there, maybe the "Sharks" at one point). Honestly, thinking back now, I remember very little about the actual matches themselves or the goals

that were scored or the saves made, and I played every year from age six until 18 and then again post-college, so there should seemingly be a lot of memories from which to choose because I loved, and still love, playing soccer.

'However, I could very easily sketch for you EVERY jersey that I wore.

'I remember each season when there was only a practice or two until the first match and the coach would pull a big cardboard box out of his car and you knew it was finally time to see the jerseys you would get to wear for the year. The box would be opened at the end of that practice and so began the rush of excitement when you would learn your colours for the year and hope that your number was available in the correct size. I'll spare everyone the chronological list, but in case you're wondering the first jersey (age six) was maroon, with a big white stripe across the middle with white shorts and maroon socks, and the next season (age seven) was the same design but with green and white. Once I started plying my trade as a goalkeeper, you better believe my fashion game truly stepped up to the next level.

'I never had enough drive though to really make anything of myself as a soccer player and living in the US there wasn't as much exposure to European soccer on TV as we have now, so it could be difficult to have more than a circumstantial relationship with the sport. However, with the 2006 men's World Cup that changed for me.

'The 1994 men's World Cup was a big deal in the US for sure and as a nine-year-old kid I was impressed, but 2006 was different. I was an adult and in Europe for the first time. I stood on a street in Paris when France beat Spain to advance to the quarter-finals. I happened to be sitting in an Italian cafe in Florence when Italy beat Germany in stoppage time to move on to the final. My walk back to the hotel that night then turned into an hours-long party in the city centre watching seemingly normal people dancing on buses. This was a soccer I had never experienced.

'Coming home from that trip I had a renewed love of soccer. I played *FIFA*, and then *Pro Evolution* and eventually back to *FIFA*, many more hours than I ever had previously. I began learning the leagues, the teams (see my obsession with Borussia Dortmund), the players, and of course the kits. Oh my, the kits.

'I would spend hours updating kits in *Pro Evo* and recreating jerseys in Photoshop (OK, it was Gimp because I was a cheap college kid) as meticulously as I could and I found great pleasure in the results, but I knew it wasn't exactly what I wanted. There was something about all my work solely existing in a memory card or a computer that ultimately wasn't satisfying; perhaps my penchant for building model cars had trained my brain for a more tactile finished product, so I began experimenting.

'First up was wood and the result was, well, fine. I truly had no idea what I was doing with regard to carving wood (I still don't), or how to make it look how I wanted. There was minimal detail and it looked like a sanded wood block with a couple of smaller sanded wood blocks slapped on the sides as sleeves. It wasn't going to work for me, so a little bit of research led me to polymer clay and the rest, as they say, is history.

'With polymer clay I could more easily create what I was visualising. If I messed up (which was often) I could either correct it fairly easily, or if it was bad enough, I could just form it back into a ball and start over. That's not to say there wasn't a learning curve with clay also, as I had no formal training and generally had no idea

what I was doing, so I made lots of mistakes. Looking back now at the few remaining sculpts from these early days, there was LOTS of room for improvement but that is also part of the draw for me. I get so much satisfaction learning new skills and finding creative ways to solve problems, but I truly love the pursuit of perfection and seeing my growth as an artist (it still feels weird calling myself an artist, sometimes).

'The first jersey I made was some time in 2012 and was the Houston Astros home jersey from around 1993. Purely based on nostalgia, it was a jersey from my childhood that I wanted to own but knew I would never actually wear. I quickly realised that soccer felt the same; teams were putting out so many amazing shirts every year and there was no way I was going to be able to own every shirt I wanted and even if I could they were just going to sit in a closet most likely, so it was in that realisation that TinyJerseys was born. It wasn't until many years later that it got a name and became more than just a personal hobby, but the existence was there.

'Since 2012, I've gone through a few different versions of the TinyJersey with many varying techniques and ideas but in 2020, version three came about and was the first time I had made the full body sculpt and I really began to make my presence known in the online community and I've kept a fairly consistent backlog ever since.'

4

Up Pohnpei

IF ANYTHING speaks to the hermetically sealed bubble that is the Premier League, it's the annual No Home Kit campaign. The top table was glacially slow in supporting the campaign (to be fair, by 2023, 17 of its clubs had taken part) but, at the base of the deceptively described 'football pyramid', the National League embraced it from the start. Starting over Christmas 2021, fans were encouraged not to wear their home kits for the Boxing Day fixtures to show solidarity for those left homeless by the Covid crisis, rising bills and a dozen miserable years of Tory misrule. Covid alone was estimated to have made almost 200,000 households homeless and the campaign was focussed on, and driven by, the charity Shelter, which connected the National League's 66 clubs involved in this elegantly simple and moving act of solidarity with those deprived of homes and losing hope. In that first year, over 100 clubs from the Premier League, EFL, and National League participated and helped to raise over £1m for Shelter, despite a raft of Covid-driven postponements. For the 2022 campaign, the wreckage wrought by the

'KamiKwarsi' mini-budget and increasingly insecure rental agreements was highlighted by the heartbreaking story of little Awaab Ishak from Rochdale who died from a respiratory condition caused by exposure to mould in his family's flat. This made the campaign even more important, and the Premier League's slow take-up increasingly tone deaf. For the 2022/23 festive period, clubs were invited to designate one of the raft of Christmas fixtures to the campaign and encourage fans to swap and donate shirts and give money to expand the campaign's reach and impact. Talking to the media, National League general manager Mark Ives shared this agonising statistic, 'Every 90 minutes, 25 households are made homeless. That is something we simply cannot ignore.'

Covid and Conservative-ruined Christmases are depressing to reflect on but, for the 2022 festive season, there was also an added layer of heartbreak. Daily atrocities meted out by Putin's henchmen made the exchange of gifts we didn't need (and often didn't want) seem pointless and perverse when so much anguish was unfolding in the heart of Europe. The feeling of powerlessness to help the poor Ukrainian families was at least eased slightly by the chance to help evicted families suffering on our, and their former, doorsteps. Ukrainians crave shelter and dignity, something we often take for granted, but for many UK families, their basic rights are cruelly denied them.

Talking to *The Independent* at the end of November 2022, football coach and activist Paul Watson felt the sport, particularly in the Premier League world, was failing kids. Paul's project started with only ten shirts stored in his garage ready to be given to children in refugee camps and parts of the world where an authentic shirt was next to impossible for most people to afford. But, when given ten new Manchester United shirts in late 2020, the idea of Kitmas took hold; it has now created huge momentum and support. The original plan was to give the shirts to a local food bank in Stroud but, after talking to his comedian brother Mark, his tweets asking who was looking to give spare shirts generated a torrent of interest and the subsequent Crowdfunder page for people who didn't have a shirt to give but wanted to contribute was the start of a three-year mission which has grown exponentially. Talking to Sky's Kay Burley in November 2022, Mark said, 'This is a way of sustainably recycling. Football is such a wasteful industry in so many ways, so expensive and so heartless in a lot of ways and this is a way of reconnecting kids with the magic of it.'

For Paul, Christmas is a catalyst for the joy of receiving football shirts as a way to support those who otherwise could not have afforded one. Over Christmas 2022, during a cost of living crisis biting hard on his neighbouring Gloucestershire families, Paul and his supporters gave away 2,000 kits as much-needed Christmas presents. With his wife, Lizzie, Paul raised over £14,000 through their Crowfunder page adding to an astonishing total of £25,000 for the year that distributed 2,025 shirts to 35 centres across the UK and Canada by the end of 2022 including, to be fair to a man often vilified and pilloried for his on-screen buffoonery, £2,000 from presenter James Corden. Talking to the

BBC's Steve Mather in late November 2022, Paul said he saw his role as taking some of the pressure off parents and giving the children 'a sense of identity'. This was the third Christmas of using shirts to help children feel this, with the first year distributing 1,000 shirts before doubling the total in 2021. By Christmas 2022, they had raised an astonishing total of £44,806.

Paul and Lizzie's incredible work was also supported by clubs including Cheltenham Town, who gave away 210 shirts to local families, and matchday shirt collections at Bristol City's Ashton Gate and my Exeter City who donated a set of kits from their famous academy system. There was even a competition via the makers of the *Football Manager* video game series that gave players the chance to win one of ten Football Manager FC shirts for those who donated their tops to the campaign.

Just when I thought I couldn't admire Paul more, in March 2023 he appeared on *The Guardian*'s *Football Weekly* podcast to share how this man from Stroud was promoting football shirt designs from Micronesia by manufacturer Stingz, with all proceeds going to pay for the cost of flights to the region's first futsal tournament. The Micro Cup featured the giants of Chuuk (population 54,000, or equivalent to South Croydon), Pohnpei (34,000 or my home town of Exmouth in Devon), Yap (population 16,000, or St Ives in Cambridgeshire) and the minnows of Kosrae with only 6,000 people living in an area the size of Bristol (which has a population 460,000 higher).

Paul, and the shirts produced, played a big part in making the tournament successful as well as breaking

new ground for many of the players. Organised in various countries each year, the tournament relies on multiple sources of funding to cover its expenses, such as travel, accommodation, and equipment for participating teams. In recent years, the introduction of shirt sales has been a valuable addition to the tournament's revenue streams that have positively impacted the Micro Cup, providing financial support, raising awareness, and fostering a sense of community among participants and fans. Traditionally, the tournament relied on ticket sales, sponsorships, and government grants as its primary sources of funding. Shirt sales have opened up a new avenue for generating revenue. In 2023 alone, the Micro Cup generated over US$10,000 (approximately £8,000) from shirt sales, which significantly contributed to covering the tournament's expenses.

The Micro Cup is a relatively small-scale tournament that faces challenges when it comes to raising awareness outside of Micronesia. Shirt sales have played a crucial role in increasing the tournament's visibility and promoting it to a wider audience. By featuring the tournament logo and the names of participating teams, the shirts themselves act as walking advertisements for the event. When fans wear these shirts, they become ambassadors for the Micro Cup, sparking conversations and piquing interest among those who may not have been aware of its existence. Additionally, the funds generated from shirt sales are allocated towards marketing and promotional activities. This includes advertisements in newspapers, magazines, and strategic social media campaigns, further amplifying the tournament's reach and impact.

But, as plenty of people must have thought: why, Paul, why? For those of you who have read Paul's book (and if you haven't I strongly recommend that you do) *Up Pohnpei*, published in 2013, he told the story of his quest to find the world's worst football team, find a way to become naturalised and play for them to complete a lifelong ambition of receiving an international 'cap'. In the book football shirts play a significant role, offering insights into the challenges faced by the Pohnpei national team and the generosity they encountered along their journey. Throughout the book, there are four notable instances where shirts are mentioned, each highlighting different aspects of the team's experiences.

In chapter one, Paul and his friend Matthew Conrad reach out to 92 Premier League and Football

League teams in England, requesting kit donations for the Pohnpei national team. Their efforts are met with positive responses from Spurs, Yeovil, and Norwich. This initial success sets the foundation for their remarkable adventure and showcases the willingness of these clubs to support the Pohnpei team. Moving ahead to chapter five, Paul and Matthew arrive in Pohnpei and meet with the national team. The players eagerly anticipate the arrival of the kit donations from England. However, their enthusiasm is dampened when they realise that there are no footballs included in the donations. This setback sheds light on the team's challenges and the limitations they face due to resource constraints, highlighting the importance of not only football shirts but also other vital equipment. In chapter 11, Paul and Matthew organise a match between the Pohnpei national team and a group of local businessmen. The game takes place on an improvised pitch, and the players proudly wear the kit donations from England. This event showcases the profound impact of the generous contributions on the team's spirit and sense of identity.

Returning to Pohnpei in chapter 13 after a year, Paul and Matthew are astonished to find the team wearing their shirts, courtesy of a local businessman's generous donation. This development symbolises the strong bond between the team and the community, emphasising the lasting impact of their collective journey.

Throughout the book, heartwarming photographs showcase the Pohnpei team proudly wearing the donated kits from England. These images capture the tangible impact of these contributions and the unity

they foster. They also highlight the local businessmen whose generosity further strengthens the connection between the team and the community, emphasising the power of kindness and support.

Yap became the eventual Micro Cup champions after defeating the surprise package Kosra 9-7 on 14 July 2023.

Paul's experiences remind me of the superb 2014 documentary *Next Goal Wins*, which starts with American Samoa's 31-0 (although some people think it may have been 32-0) capitulation to Australia in a World Cup qualification match in 2001. 'Challenging' does an awful lot of heavy lifting in every sentence. American Samoa's Football Federation chairman Tavita Taumua bemoans how the world considers his players to be part of 'a fast-food team'. Having never won a competitive game, we can only warm to the blind optimism of Tavita's comment that 'Rome was not built in a day'.

Midfielder Pati Sinapati shows the magic of football and its aspirations when he says, 'Success for us is working as a team. Win or lose as long as the world knows American Samoa will never give up.' Volunteer coach Larry Mana'o pinpointed the key reason why so many coaches had failed to lift the team out of their doldrums, 'A lot of people have tried to come over here and help them. They do it technically correct. The problem is that they then have to understand the Samoan culture.' Preparing for the 2011 South Pacific Games, their first tournament in four years, they were looking to overcome other FIFA minnows Fiji (ranked 158 going into the tournament), New Caledonia (163) and New Guinea (190). American Samoa were bottom of the global pile in 204th. Hopes were high when arriving at Noumea, New Caledonia. It didn't go well. Even Tavita Taumua couldn't put a positive spin on 26 goals conceded and none scored.

One month before the next round of World Cup qualifiers, enter stage left their own Paul Watson, Thomas Rongen. Overcoming the other candidates (a field of precisely zero), Rongen seemed to be indulging in a case of wilful career suicide. But something clicked. Rongen had already coached a dozen teams starting from the CV padding at Pope John Paul II High School, but, more impressively, he'd had two stints with the US under-20 team. Standing in the way of American Samoan World Cup glory in Brazil at the

2014 tournament were the Cook Islands, Tonga and Samoa. They had never even scored against any of them. Ferociously motivated by the tragic death of his daughter Nicole on the way to university, the openness of addressing this heartbreaking tragedy began to build morale among the 'world's worst team'. He and his wife Gail adopted a mantra from his late daughter to drive both them and their new team forward, 'Anything is possible. You just have to find a way to make it happen.'

For Paul, the need from the Pohnpei Football Association was also for leadership. As his book relates, he was charged with organising their first fixture since a demoralising 16-1 reverse several years earlier. I won't give away the ending, but a decade later Paul still feels the pull of Pohnpei. The shirts only cost £30 and the take-up was astonishing, with jaded shirt buyers used to ridiculous costs (Scotland's 150th anniversary boxed shirt for £150, anyone?) blindsided by blissful footballing purity. Paul's tweets narrated a tapestry of tantalising tales for shirts that, beautifully and sensitively designed, cost so little and helped so much. For example, the Bristol of Micronesia, Kosrae, had never had a shirt of their own before and this tournament was their first chance to show off their design of the Kosrae white-eye, a bird unique to the island, while Paul's Pohnpei shirts celebrated the coconut cup used for the traditional Sakau ceremony on the island. In our cynical world of shirt sales, there is still space for the hopeful romantic determined to create change for good.

5

Nairn County: Honed by Heartbreak

HIGHLAND LEAGUE club Nairn County showed a shirt's power to catalyse grief prefacing hope in August 2022. They gave their third XI shirt over to TeamHamish, a local charity set up by Sam and Susan Hey as, like the Adam Stansfield Foundation, a legacy for their son who died in 2017 at the heartbreaking age of eight. To add to the family's despair, by the time they were ready to open a play area known as Hamish's Splashpad, Susan had lost her battle with cancer. A sum of £10 from every sale of an adult shirt and £5 from every junior shirt went to TeamHamish and the vibrant, multi-coloured

chevrons were a tribute to Susan's favourite dress. The
club went on to raise £3,356.50 for TeamHamish in the
2022/23 season through shirts, donations and charity
matches. I was delighted to get in touch with the kit's
originator, Michael Bochel, in late 2022 and his passion,
determination and innovation allowed the shirt's story
to flourish and resonate.

Let's hand it over to Michael to tell us more, 'Up until working with Nairn, I have only been involved in launching kits. It was quite the experience going through it all from design to manufacturing and then launch. As a club, unless there is a change in sponsor, we are committed to keeping our kit for two seasons. The way we see it, we are a non-league club. It doesn't make any sense to us for our fans to change kits every season. When I joined, we were going through the second season of our kits and it turned out the final year of sponsorship with our main sponsors, due to a takeover at their end. Historically, we have had shirts made by the usual suspects – Nike, Adidas and more recently, Puma. They did a bespoke away kit for us that featured all the names of the players who helped us win our first ever trophy as a club back in 1920. However, with the pandemic as a contributing factor, they were scaling back their operations in the north of Scotland, so we were going to be on the hunt for a new supplier.

'When I joined the club, I wanted to do more things that brought the club closer to the town. One way was to have a bespoke kit that was heavily inspired by the town. The idea was to have a home shirt that featured the Bandstand, which is a landmark in Nairn that anyone from the town would recognise, and the away shirt to feature every street name in the IV12 postcode, which covers the Nairn area. We had a third kit the previous season and while not every club at our level had one, I felt there was a lot of potential to do something very special with this kit and make it a charity third design. I'd seen some examples of this with other clubs and, for me, if we were going to do it, there was only one charity I wanted to try it with. TeamHamish. The thinking with the third kit was that if we could help shine a spotlight in any way on the charity and fundraise for their phase two plans, we wanted to do it.

'Greenock Morton fan and part-time concept kit designer Gavin Macintosh helped with the designs of all three. For TeamHamish's third kit, it is no exaggeration when I say how Gavin absolutely smashed the brief the first time of asking. Using the information I had given him about the charity and pictures of the splashpad and Nairn, he went and did his own research. He found a picture of Susan in one of her favourite dresses and designed the shirt we have today. Straight off the bat, we knew as soon as we saw it that it was the one. But, of course, we only had the designs. We still needed a kit manufacturer, so I reached out to Hope and Glory. Ric Dennis, who started it, went above and beyond on more than one occasion to make sure we had our

kit, including when we hit issues with sponsor logos. However, we still had the third kit to deal with. All we had was an image file rather than an appropriate file type that we needed and there was no guarantee that the vibrancy of the rainbow design would come through. Speaking to a couple of people that had done bespoke kits before, I took a calculated risk and signed off on the designs. The third kit didn't launch until mid-August due to the timing of getting the kit made and sent over.

'In the past, for photoshoots, we had just used players at the ground, but for this one and the special nature of it all, I wanted to do something a bit different. I lined up a mate who had two young kids aged five and seven, [and] a couple of his teenage staff to be part of the photoshoot and after speaking to Sam at TeamHamish and asking Hamish's sister (who also got involved which brought it completely together) we then added three of our own young local players. That all took place at the splashpad and Nairn beach. When we launched, the response from the local community, football fans and non-football fans was unbelievable. Timings worked out well, coinciding with the Nairn Highland Games where we had a stall and could sell it. I sent out press releases to local and national papers at 10am on the day of the launch and the local STV news. We sold out by lunchtime of game day. In all the years of selling kits, the club has never sold out in such a short space of time. We were cautious with how much we originally ordered but, in hindsight, we should have had faith in just how special this kit was. Our second order was huge in comparison with a view to Christmas and a dedicated league match for TeamHamish.

'The aim for me was to have three kits that resonated with the town and I'm happy to report that all three have done just that.'

I am one of their proud customers and the shirt certainly turns heads in the gym. It is unapologetically bold, life-affirming and unique. Just what any kit design should speak to. There was no let-up in 2023 for the club's support of TeamHamish either. As of March 2023, Nairn County FC has raised over £3,350. The club committed to continuing its fundraising efforts in the future and held a match against Elgin City on 2 April 2023, with all proceeds going to TeamHamish. The power of a shirt to ease the hurt.

6

We Wear Because We Care

SOME 30 miles south-west of Nairn, I also had the pleasure of talking to Marty Mainland to hear the passion he has not only for Loch Ness FC as a player with his twin, Craig, but for his designs of their kits. As Marty's Designs Ltd he has worked with the North Caledonian FA, but I was intrigued to learn more about the club that clearly means so much to him. Playing in the North Caledonian League, the second tier of Scottish football, where they finished second in 2022, 2023 saw them celebrate their first quarter of a century after being founded in 1999 by current manager Shane Carling – and a title-winning season.

Loch Ness are no strangers to making waves with their kit design. Their 2020 creation featuring Nessie front and centre won several awards and even inspired *Match of the Day*'s Gary Lineker to tweet pictures of the kit and describe it as 'one of the BEST football shirts we have ever seen!' The resulting global sales were a tremendous boost to the coffers, but coming just before the Covid-19 lockdowns it also averted an existential

club crisis at a time of zero alternative income. It's easy to dismiss football shirts for smaller clubs as either ephemeral headline-grabbers with sometimes outrageous designs (like Sporting Braga's bizarre Roman armour kit, or Spanish club La Hoya Lorca's 2013 frozen pea third kit), or dust-gatherers with a short shelf life and little inspiration. On holiday in Slovakia in 2022, I went to the local team where we were staying at Nitra FC. Their 'kits' were separated into their component parts of a plain base layer with the badge, sponsor logos

and league badge lying beleaguered in boxes behind the heat press, like so many forgotten former favourite toys. There was something desperately dispiriting about a kit that had to be begrudgingly assembled rather than being a proud symbol of a club's values and personality. They were relegated that season from the Fortuna Liga, so maybe karma was working its magic.

In 2021 Loch Ness FC announced a three-year kit deal with Lancashire-based Zero Negativity, an eco-friendly supplier that used eight recycled plastic bottles to make each shirt. But it's not only the kit components that serve their values-driven principles. Their printing uses water-based inks instead of plastic. Even their embroidery uses specialised, organic threads. I try to teach my students about how a business culture defines 'how we do things around here', and Zero Negativity practise exactly what they preach. Even the name reflects their determination to create zero negativity for the environment, which also covers recycled packaging, renewable green energy in their offices and a commitment to only accept customers who adhere to the same environmental principles as them. For the chosen customers, orders even come with detailed reports summarising their order's water, energy, plastic and CO_2 savings.

It's fantastic to report on the massive strides they made in 2023. One of their key achievements was a partnership with Manchester City, announced in March 2023, to develop a sustainable kit for the upcoming 2023/24 season. This innovative kit was manufactured using recycled materials and was carbon neutral, showcasing the company's commitment to environmental responsibility. In April 2023, Zero Negativity expanded their sustainable product range by introducing a new line of football boots. Made from recycled materials, they are not only eco-friendly but also vegan-friendly, appealing to a wider audience of environmentally conscious athletes. Zero Negativity gained further recognition in May 2023 when they were featured in a BBC documentary centred around sustainable football. The programme highlighted the company's mission to create environmentally friendly kits and boots and shed light on their efforts to drive positive change within the industry. They have even partnered with the United Nations Environment Programme to advocate for sustainable football practices and are proud members of the Sustainable Apparel Coalition, a collective of businesses striving to enhance the sustainability of the apparel industry.

People like Marty show that the bloated behemoths at football's top table using shirts to promote Asian-facing gambling sites routed through unregulated white-label companies in tax havens don't have to win every time. Buying a Loch Ness shirt that calls on us to share in a values-driven community is a small win for football but a bigger one for the society we aspire to belong to. If karma is indeed working its magic, the new partnership for the 2023/24 season marks a huge uplift in scale and

quality that gives us hope that might is not always right. While Nessie was more muted for the 2023/24 design by the new design partners, Edinburgh-based Appin, she circled both sleeves and cheekily peaked from above the club crest. Life is short. Buy the shirt.

* * *

Project 35

As an Exeter City season ticket holder, let's get this one out of the way. Our fierce 'El Pastyco' rivals Plymouth Argyle have just completed a dozen-year shirt front partnership with tasty local pasty makers Ginsters. The fear is always that the sponsorship void will be filled with unregulated and speculative online casinos and NFTs offering bell curve of doom returns, but Argyle have chosen a far more satisfying route. For the 2022/23 season, and running for at least three seasons, the Pilgrims were sponsored by the community social impact initiative Project 35. This continued the long-standing connection with Ginsters, but the pasty makers stepped away from the shirt and supported the club through the lens of social inclusion.

In January 2023, the club produced their first Community Trust Impact Report about the shirts and the high profile Project 35 had helped to promote and drive. The Plymouth Argyle Community Trust's programmes reached over 20,000 people in the 2021/22 season. They had a positive impact on participants' physical and mental health, as well as their social skills and confidence, and helped reduce social isolation and promote inclusion, particularly for young people from disadvantaged backgrounds. The trust's programmes helped improve educational attainment and employment prospects for young people and were highly valued by participants, with 90 per cent of respondents saying that they would recommend them to others. People appreciated the opportunity to participate in sports activities, learn new skills, and make new friends. They also valued the support and guidance that they received from the trust's staff. The report also found that the trust's programmes were cost-effective, with every £1 invested them generating £3.50 in social value.

Overall, the Community Trust Impact Report found that the trust's programmes are having a positive impact on the lives of people in Plymouth, helping improve physical and mental health, social skills and confidence, educational attainment and employment prospects. The trust's work is also helping to reduce social isolation and promote inclusion. There is nothing

for it but to doff my red and white cap to our Devonian neighbours. It is deeply satisfying to report that, when the kit for the 2023/24 season was unveiled on 1 July 2023 after Argyle won promotion to the madman's casino of the Championship, they chose not to join the sordid stampede for the dying embers of gambling shirt sponsorship and continued to promote Project 35. The key focus of Plymouth's new partnership is to highlight the pernicious poverty blighting areas of the city using a wide-ranging approach spanning, as the Argyle media team describes it, 'fundraising, awareness raising, social outreach, food donations, education, and charity support'.

The reason for the project's title is that an estimated 35 per cent of children in Plymouth were recorded (in the latest research from 2019) to be living in poverty. Clearly, with the pandemic, cost of living crisis and soaring inflation, this number is likely to be even higher by now. The initiative aims to raise awareness, but its key focus is on taking action. Free meals will be offered to children from the most badly affected areas of the city during school holidays (look away those MPs who voted against it). Project 35 also provides weekend hampers and makes food appeals at Argyle matches where fans home and away can leave their gifts at dedicated donation points around the stadium. As well as tangible relief, the project will also focus on providing emotional and educational support to families battered by horrifically harsh economic headwinds. The catalyst for all these laudable actions was front and centre of shirts for the men, women and academy teams. A heartening initiative in an often cynical fabric billboard.

For my Exeter City, their third kit for the 2023/24 season also spoke to their values and sense of community. Celebrating two decades of trust ownership that rescued them from non-league football (and the Michael Jackson/Uri Geller circus), the classy black design was sponsored front and centre by the supporters' trust and a circle on the back also celebrated '20 Years Supporter Owned'. The partnership was only for a single season, but it meant that Devon's two biggest clubs had committed to support, celebrate and share the values that so many other shirts had abandoned for one last hit of the dark money showered down by gambling companies and the murder of shysters schilling NFTs and crypto.

Nick Hawker, chair of the Exeter City Supporters' Trust shared with the in-house media team the ethical stance that underpins the club, 'Through this sponsorship we want to demonstrate how a supporter-owned club can be sustainably and successfully run and we know people will wear them with great pride in their club.

'We randomly selected 20 trust members who have been members since before the trust purchased the club to receive this year's third shirt to thank them for their long-standing membership and to celebrate the longevity of our fan ownership.'

There is hope yet.

* * *

Exeter Strollers Football Club – a legacy of community and sportsmanship

Exeter Strollers Football Club, nestled in the heart of Exeter, England, stands as a testament to the enduring power of community and sportsmanship. Founded in 2018, the club has swiftly garnered a reputation for its welcoming atmosphere, fostering a passion for football among individuals of all ages and skill levels.

Beyond the thrill of competition, Exeter Strollers embodies the true spirit of camaraderie, where players unite under a shared love for the beautiful game. The club's walking football teams, catering to both men and women over the age of 40, provide a haven for those seeking to rekindle their passion for football at a more leisurely pace.

Exeter Strollers' commitment to inclusivity extends beyond the pitch, as the club actively organises social events, fostering a sense of belonging among its members. These gatherings, ranging from casual pints at the clubhouse to lively team dinners, serve as a platform for players to connect beyond the confines of the football field.

The club's dedication to its community is further exemplified by its active participation in local events and initiatives. Exeter Strollers has established itself as a cornerstone of the Exeter sporting scene, regularly hosting tournaments, workshops, and training sessions, always eager to share its passion for football with others.

The club's unwavering commitment to inclusivity, camaraderie, and community outreach has undoubtedly left an indelible mark on the sporting landscape of Exeter.

Beyond the visual appeal, Exeter Strollers' bespoke designed shirts contribute deeply to a profound sense of community.

The shared symbol on the shirts creates a visual marker of belonging, uniting players under a common banner and fostering a sense of shared identity. It allows them to stand out as a team, differentiating themselves from other clubs and forging a unique identity.

Donning the shirts instils each member's pride and belonging, fostering camaraderie and a collective spirit. It is a constant reminder of their shared passion for the sport and their commitment to the club.

The shirts act as a tangible reminder of the shared experience and values of the club, strengthening the bonds between players both on and off the field. It generates a sense of solidarity and interconnectedness, making each member feel like a valuable part of something bigger than themselves.

Lastly, the design creates a unique and memorable symbol of the club, etching cherished memories for every member. Looking back at these shirts in the years to come will evoke a sense of nostalgia and ignite fond memories of shared experiences within the community.

* * *

Another great example of sponsors side-stepping shirt profile came in Scotland. Kits can share a meaningful message at one step removed if the original sponsor is empathetic and flexible. For the 2021/22 season, Edinburgh's Heart of Midlothian played with MND Scotland on the front of their shirts in memory of former captain Marius Žaliūkas who died of motor neurone disease, a vicious progressive neurological condition that affects the brain and spinal cord. The club had started a two-year shirt sponsorship deal with computer giants Dell Technologies, who moved their logo to the back of the shirts and funded the MND Scotland promotion, while Hearts contributed to the charity for every shirt sold. A fantastic figure of over £130,000 was eventually raised through the partnership and fed into the charity's MND Awareness Week and a fundraising, awareness-raising charity match attended by over 20,000 fans that raised over £100,000. This led to the creation of an MND support group for fans affected by MND or who know someone who is. The group

provides a forum for fans to share their experiences and offer support to each other.

A kit's power to serve a higher purpose came in 2017. Portugal's Sporting Lisbon released their home kit which included a Morse code and braille message underneath the club crest. The message was also stamped into the away jersey and exhorted fans, all fans, on what to give and expect to receive back from the club, 'Effort, Dedication, Devotion and Glory'.

Adding to the beautiful inclusion, manufacturers Macron designed horizontal stripes that, represented in Morse code, described a favourite chant of the Lions. This is yet another example of a shirt's huge potential to reach out to all supporters and show them they are part of the football family. History resides in them, not

the transient owners. This compelling collegiality also reflects badly on so many clubs choosing to phone in designs to produce pedestrian shirts that were created by an artistic hive of inactivity and say nothing more to us than how much we are prepared to pay for them.

This idea would be picked up with a twist for the Aston Villa home kit in the 2023/24 season. The soundwaves on the home shirt were a subtle print of soundwaves taken from fans singing the club's 'Allez, Allez, Allez' chant. They were created by a team of sound engineers who had recorded the chant at a match. They then used software to extract the soundwaves from the recording and to create a digital file that could be printed on to the kit. The soundwaves are printed in a subtle grayscale pattern that is only visible when the shirt is held up to the light.

Shirts can also transcend the superficial stories of fashion and planned obsolescence, as demonstrated by the mighty Lionesses.

* * *

England and Australia women's teams unite to raise dementia awareness

On 11 April 2023, the England and Australia women's teams played a remarkable international friendly that captured the attention and hearts of fans worldwide. In a unique display of solidarity and compassion, a third of the players from each team wore shirts without names to raise awareness of dementia, a debilitating neurodegenerative disorder. Additionally, the shirts proudly displayed the Alzheimer's Society logo, further amplifying the cause. Dementia is a prevalent condition that affects millions of people worldwide. In the United Kingdom alone, one in three people born will develop dementia, according to the Alzheimer's Society, impairing memory, thinking, and behaviour, making it challenging for sufferers to carry out their daily activities independently. The effects of dementia extend beyond the individual, impacting families and communities.

During the half-time break, the players exchanged their shirts, ensuring that everyone had the opportunity to experience playing with a nameless shirt. This helped create awareness about the confusion and memory loss often experienced by people living with dementia. By immersing themselves in the unique perspective of those affected, the players fostered empathy and understanding among television spectators and stadium supporters.

The poignant match took place at the Brentford Community Stadium in London, where the vibrant atmosphere and shared passion for the cause added to the significance of the event. The occasion ended with a 2-2 draw, highlighting the spirit of unity and equality on the field. The Alzheimer's Society commended the teams for their remarkable gesture and support of its cause. By using their platform to raise awareness of dementia, the players demonstrated their commitment to making a positive difference in the lives of those affected by this devastating condition. The kits served as a powerful catalyst for increased public awareness and sparked conversations about the importance of research into dementia. The match received overwhelming support from fans who took to social media platforms to express their admiration for the initiative and gratitude towards the players. The heartfelt gestures displayed by the teams resonated deeply with those who had personal experiences with dementia or knew someone affected by the condition. The collective outpouring of support helped spread the message far and wide, inspiring others to join the cause.

But not all worthy efforts using kits to support causes pass the design test. After I wrote in *Kit and Caboodle* about the enlightened approach by League of Ireland Premier Division club Bohemians, who used their shirts to welcome refugees and celebrate Bob Marley's concert at Dalymount Park in 1980, Bohs, well, parked the bus for the 2022/23 season. Although an off-the-wall decision, the kits continued to raise awareness and funds using the Bohemians Community Trust were disbursed for important causes with ten per cent of sales donated to LGBT Ireland and ShoutOut, a charity that takes the message of tolerance and inclusion for LGBTQ+ people into schools with tailored education programmes. The trust would go on to donate €15,000 to LGBT Ireland and ShoutOut in 2023 through sales of the shirts.

The Marley and Refugees Welcome shirts were easy to enjoy, but this one is certainly challenging to the initial onlooker. For most of us, considering this design riffing on that of bus seat covers (the kit also features the logos of both Bohemians and the Dublin Bus Company), it conjures up images of rancid chewing gum, slashed seats and dark stains that don't bear thinking about. Worn for the FAI Cup, it was a collaboration, not surprisingly, with the Dublin Bus Company. As ever when a club decides to push the creative boundaries, there was plenty of online pushback. For one Twitter warrior (appropriately with an account handle of 'GrumpyAulFella') this design decision further showed how 'the club needs to worry about football first. The social and humanitarian aid work should take a back seat until affairs are sorted on the pitch. It's a football club after all, not Barnardos.' Ouch.

* * *

Still no more red

Far too often in our attention-fractured lives, worthy campaigns enter in a blaze of publicity, flare fleetingly then fade away. But, as I shared in *Kit and Caboodle*, Arsenal have kept faith with their No More Red campaign and shown how continued spotlight can attract tangible rewards. In 2022 the club introduced a narrative of hope over hate. This included No More Red Social Action Projects where 30 young people took part in creating a No More Red mural in Rosemary Gardens, Islington, a football pitch on the Harvist Estate neighbouring the Emirates was refurbished, and role models from the local community like boxer Anthony Yarde gave their time and stories freely to the project. 2023 broadened the campaign's horizon and built on the foundations laid. The focus also widened to include Arsenal Women, who used the local derby against Chelsea on 15 January to wear all-white pre-match jackets. The men would wear the shirts against Spurs in January 2023 which played a part in raising an astonishing £250,000 to support the charity in that year alone.

Despite the horrific consequences of knife crime continuing to ripple through the lives of the young, thanks to initiatives like No More Red there was a significant drop in incidents during 2022, but there were still 11,500 reported knife crimes in London during the year. We can assume that many go unreported by victims fearing reprisals for contacting the police. But when the choice is between doing something or nothing, affirmative action always needs to be seen as the right decision.

The stage was again the FA Cup third round (with a much better outcome than when they unveiled the white kit against Nottingham Forest the previous season). The focus changed slightly. Whereas the first campaign rewarded people running organisations aiming to address the blight of knife crime, the second iteration sought members of the public to buy into, and volunteer for, one of their established charity partners. Instead of the original gifting of 20 shirts, now they had a wider but still campaign-focussed remit to get the white shirt message out to the communities struggling with such heartbreak and wasted lives. Each of the assigned charities was offered ten shirts to share with volunteers, keeping the scarcity and value high and allowing them to reward the best beacons of hope with the coveted shirt based on the time they invested in the project. Keeping to first principles, the shirt remains unavailable to buy (non-fakes at least).

But, before we reach out to touch the Arsenal halo, let's go back to John Nicholson who, writing for Football365 on 26 June 2023, nailed the madness of the Gunners' latest shirt price point in an article with the eviscerating title, 'Arsenal, the £110 new shirt and the nonsense of a price that takes the absolute p***'.

'Is a football shirt worth £110? Arsenal are about to find out, once they've fixed a design error which led to their new version withdrawal last week. There has long been a move to reposition official replica shirts as upmarket "designer" fashion wear, going back to the mid-90s when Newcastle United launched an away strip that was a kind of denim colour – so you could match it with your Joe Bloggs jeans, presumably. Fans of free market capitalism will inevitably say that if you don't want to pay £110 you don't have to (and there is an £80 "fan" version on offer from Arsenal). While this is obviously true, other forces are in play.

'Premier League football clubs are not normal businesses which have to make profits to survive. For a start, they are given about £150m of free money every year. That doesn't happen in any other business. And if no one buys the shirt, they don't care because shirt sales don't generate much profit in the first place. The old "they'll pay for the transfer fee with shirt sales alone" idea is a complete myth. The Sports Journal [a website covering various sporting topics] looked into this earlier in the year and concluded that if a club sells 100,000 shirts throughout a season, sales of a £75 shirt would generate a total revenue of £7.5m, of which a club would typically receive a 7.5 per cent fee. Therefore, the commission earned by the club would be a little over £562,000.

'Manchester United are the best sellers, shifting 2.55 million shirts last year and pulled in £106m from those sales. If they're on 7.5 per cent, they've made a little over £7m as part of an approximately £700m turnover. They have 11 players on their books who earn more than that in a year, four of which earn more than double. Arsenal sold 750,000 shirts costing £77.3m; that's under £6m in commission if they're on the typical 7.5 per cent. If they match those sales with the £110 shirt, their cut of the £82.5m generated takes them just over £6m, which is less than half what they pay Gabriel Jesus alone.

'The people making the money are the companies in between the factory and the store. Understandably, fans think they're putting money into the club coffers by buying the shirt, but most of it is going to the likes of Nike or Adidas and not the people manufacturing the shirts in factories somewhere that isn't here.

'The real value in shirts is the branding and sponsorship opportunities, so is the bad publicity charging £110 for a football shirt creates, especially in a time of economic gloom, really worth enduring for the revenue it will generate? Wouldn't it be better to stop farming it out to such people as Nike et al, go directly to the manufacturer, commission the production, buy the shirts at cost – which is thought not to exceed £5 – and sell them for a reasonable £15? Or better still, give them away for free and make up the shortfall in revenue by charging more to sponsors on the basis that they'd be seen and worn by many more people.

'Down the pyramid, smaller clubs with smaller fan bases need whatever revenue is generated from shirt sales. Their economic situation is entirely different to the Premier League teams. The shirt is more important to fans than pretty much anything else. It is all part of the brand of the club. Everything and everyone else in football comes and goes, but the shirt is always there, which is why fans get annoyed when the shirt changes markedly. This is culture and heritage and the latest dumb owner who thinks football is showbusiness messes with it at their peril. Asking over £100 suggests the underlying assumption is that the more you pay, the more it shows you care. Your loyalty is just another commodity to monetise.

'Can't clubs like Arsenal see how bad the optics are when they're furiously pulling on the udders of their fans, to milk as much as possible out of them, for something which is the very symbol of the club, the symbol of their loyalty, just to generate a small amount of profit? It makes no sense, seems very outmoded as a business model in 2023 and fails to see the bigger picture. They deserve a mighty kicking from their fans for indulging in this rip-off, a rip-off that they don't even really benefit much from.

'Former Aston Villa stalwart Olof Mellberg coached Swedish Allsvenskan League side Brommapojkarna (if you think that name is a mouthful, try their full title of Idrottsföreningen Brommapojkarna), who took the idea of scarcity one step further at the end of 2022. Their sumptuous shirt design only increases in elegance by being sponsor-free. Celebrating the club's eightieth anniversary with design partners Nike and British bespoke kit creators Stadium, it was available through an auction in September 2022. This values-driven club has over 4,000 players, mostly in youth teams, and often nurtures players who go on to play in Europe's elite leagues. A quarter of the players are female and the club is widely respected for its stance on providing equal opportunities for men and women. Worn for only one weekend in late August 2022, only two shirts were made available through the auction after being worn by the captains of the men's and women's teams. All proceeds from the jersey auction that sold for an impressive €25,000 went to support the further development of their youth system.'

* * *

Her Game Too

Wednesday, 8 March 2023 was the perfect chance for footballers, both men and women, to use their shirts to celebrate the women who inspired and supported them. International Women's Day was given an extra boost by a government decision that day to commit to equal football access for both boys and girls in school PE. I had to check my calendar that it was 2023, not 1973, when footy access equality had to be legislated for, but at least it was better (very) late than never. This move was inspired by an open letter from the Lionesses after their Euro 2022 triumph and showed the power of success to create a small spark of life in even the most moribund of governments. A key plank of the decision was to award those schools that offered parity of provision for both genders a quality Kitemark so they could be seen as a beacon of good practice.

To mark the day, FC United of Manchester unveiled a kit to be worn in the 2023/24 season by their women's team designed by New Balance Team Sports that used the palette of the purple, green and white sashes worn by the suffragette movement a century earlier. The home shirt had a purple collar and cuffs, with green stripes running down the front and back. The away shirt was white with green stripes, and the third shirt was black with green accents. All three shirts featured the logo of the Pankhurst Centre, a Manchester-based organisation that works to promote the history and legacy of the suffragette movement. The kit was worn by the FC United women's team against Manchester City Women's Academy. The match was a sell-out, and all proceeds from the ticket sales were donated to the Pankhurst Centre. I used to work with their chief executive officer Natalie Atkinson at Fair Game and she also works as director and campaign advisor for Her Game Too, so it was no surprise to see her support for such an important message. The sash design running from the right shoulder looks stunning. New Balance invoked a Wimbledon tennis vibe for a club based in a city that was front and centre of parades and rallies in support of the suffrage movement. Natalie shared with the club media team, 'I'm delighted we are able to share this exciting news on International Women's Day and lead the way for women in sport. This is a first for FC United, whereby our women's team will have their own unique kit and it feels even more special that the kit's design recognises the contributions and success of women in sport and wider society over the last century.'

Tied in with this bold statement of support, part of the proceeds were given to Manchester Women's Aid, which provides support to women and children experiencing domestic abuse. The power of shirts to be bold and hold values yet again.

The week before, neighbours Manchester City also announced their celebration of women for their Women's Super League team. Designed by Puma and featuring the club's traditional colours of sky blue and white, the home shirt had a white collar and cuffs, with sky blue stripes running down the front and back. The away shirt was white with sky blue stripes, and the third shirt was black with sky blue accents. All three shirts feature the logo of the club's women's team, as well as

the words 'Celebrating Women in Football'. The kit was officially unveiled for a sold-out match against Everton Women and all proceeds from the ticket sales were donated to the Manchester City Foundation, the club's official charity, while the men's team wore it in their

warm-up for their match against Newcastle United. This was one event for the club's 'Same City, Same Passion' campaign that merged the men's and women's team Twitter accounts, and had a dedicated weekend to promote the idea that there is no men's or women's football, just football.

For West Ham in March 2023, it was a chance to use their UEFA Europa Conference League last-16 first leg against AEK Larnaca to wear training tops with the name of women who had inspired them on the back (often their mums, of course, with 15 players doing it). For Michail Antonio it was a chance to recognise tennis legend Serena Williams as his inspirational figure, and speaking of his own decision, Declan Rice said, 'I chose to put my mum's name on the back of my shirt for training, showing my appreciation for all the time and effort she spent helping my two brothers and I become the men we are today. We will each always be forever grateful to her.'

The initiative was part of West Ham United's #WeAreThePower campaign, which aims to promote gender equality and celebrate the achievements of women. The club also aims to use its platform to support important causes and to make a positive impact on the lives of others and shirts are the perfect canvas to paint these pictures of parity.

7

Grassroot Soccer

HAVING GROWN up in Africa, anything involving the continent tugs at my heartstrings, especially when it uses football to help improve the lives of people in heartbreaking situations. That's why I was so happy to connect with Ethan McCoy, the senior manager of marketing and communications for Grassroot Soccer. Even before we spoke, I had read about an extremely high-profile supporter of their outreach work. When Bill Gates tweets about your organisation, you must have done something right.

Gates wrote, 'What makes soccer even more beautiful is the positive impact it can have off the field. There may be no better example of this than the work of a unique non-profit organisation called Grassroot Soccer. Grassroot Soccer is an adolescent health organisation that leverages the power of soccer to equip young people with the life-saving information, services, and mentorship they need to live healthier lives.'

Writing on his blog, Gates Notes, on 15 December 2022, the Microsoft co-founder shared in more detail

what makes the organisation so special, 'For the last two decades, Grassroot Soccer has used the incredible popularity of the game to help young people across Africa navigate some of their toughest health challenges … Solving these challenges is difficult – and especially important given that 60 per cent of Africans are under the age of 25. So, how can soccer make a difference? Because it's so popular, soccer offers a hook to capture the attention of young people. Grassroot Soccer uses the game to involve them in activities that encourage them to live healthier, more productive lives.'

I then handed over to Ethan for his perspective, 'Led by trained young adult "coaches" who themselves are from the communities where they work, Grassroot Soccer's evidence-based "SKILLZ" programmes incorporate soccer and fun into interactive and dynamic activities about health that engage young people and break down stigma and cultural barriers. Since it was founded in 2002, Grassroot Soccer has established itself as a game-changer in adolescent health by empowering young people to make educated choices about their most pressing and interconnected health challenges, including HIV/Aids, mental health, sexual and reproductive health and rights, gender-based violence, malaria, and, most recently, Covid-19. Grassroot Soccer works with affiliate sites in South Africa and Zambia and has also partnered with organisations in more than 60 countries, with a focus on reaching youth across sub-Saharan Africa. With proven results and a consistent focus on research and innovation, Grassroot Soccer programmes have reached more than 18 million young people, building their assets (health knowledge and the confidence to use it), improving their access to high-quality health services, and increasing their adherence to crucial treatments and healthy behaviours.'

I first heard about the organisation through Icarus, who designed my *Kit and Caboodle* shirts and provided such a superb experience that my bank account has been regularly rinsed ever since. It was the stunning Grassroot Soccer design for their 20th anniversary commemorative shirt that drew me to the organisation but, the more I learned, the more this shirt spoke to the values they stand for and ones I aspire to be associated with. Describing themselves as a 'non-profit that leverages the power of soccer to equip young people with the life-saving information, services, and mentorship they need to live healthier lives', they already had me onside. This shirt was designed to celebrate their 20th anniversary and, true to their values, all proceeds were sent to support adolescent health through football. As a man who grew up in Malawi, Central Africa, the pattern and trim inspired by traditional Xhosa patterns from South Africa (where Grassroot Soccer has a long-standing affiliate site and runs programmes) immediately attracted me and the colourful number 20 on the back to celebrate their age only adds to the feeling of fun, vibrant African culture and an affirmation of everything life-affirming this organisation aspires to.

Ethan continues, 'When designing the shirt, it was critical to Grassroot Soccer to have a design that was vibrant and fun because those elements are so central to the organisation's unique approach to working

with young people. By using soccer games that are high energy, interactive, and participatory, Grassroot Soccer makes learning fun so that young people are truly engaged, and the lessons stick. This is especially important when dealing with heavy, challenging, and often taboo health topics like HIV and mental health. When watching a Grassroot Soccer coach run a session

with young people, smiles, laughter, and dancing are all common sights – things that are not typically associated with health education.'

The kit was debuted to the world at Grassroot Soccer's 2022 World Aids Day Gala, where Dr Tommy Clark, the organisation's founder and CEO, said, 'At Grassroot Soccer, we understand how important soccer can be for young people. It's a source of inspiration, it's something that brings people together, and it's fun. Sometimes I think that is overlooked, especially when working with young people – the importance of fun. It's not a nice to have, it's a necessity.'

At the gala, the shirt impressed many of the high-profile guests and speakers in attendance, including US women's team stars and World Cup winners Christen Press and Tobin Heath, along with the popular late-night television host Seth Meyers, Angel City FC founder and president Julie Uhrman, and Major League Soccer commissioner Don Garber.

'This kit embodies the spirit of Grassroot Soccer,' said Press, who also serves on the organisation's board of directors and as a global ambassador. 'We're dealing with challenges and hard things, like health issues and lack of access to resources, but we do it in a fun way.'

When shown the shirt for the first time, Heath said, 'It screams vibrant, it screams colourful, it screams energy. Grassroot Soccer is something that everyone should be really proud to wear around and tell people about.'

Looking more closely at the shirt's crest, it is made up of 20 stars combined with a football circled by a red ribbon, the symbol of awareness and support for people living with HIV. The background of vertical black lines celebrates Highlanders FC, the club in Bulawayo, Zimbabwe, that Clark and Grassroot Soccer's three other co-founders played for during the height of the Aids epidemic. Their experience of watching friends die of Aids while playing for Highlanders led them to recognise that soccer – a positive force in the community – could be used to engage adolescents to stop the spread of HIV, leading to the founding of the organisation.

'I'm a kit fanatic and love all things soccer and fashion,' said Ethan Zohn, one of Grassroot Soccer's

co-founders and the winner of CBS's *Survivor: Africa*, in an interview with SOCCER.com. 'I have always wanted to design a jersey for Grassroot Soccer, and we had so much fun partnering with Icarus FC and creating the first official jersey for the organisation. I'm so proud of this jersey and would love to see as many soccer players, clubs, and fans as possible rocking it and representing GRS around the world!'

Unlike the latest ephemeral iteration from a Premier League behemoth hoovering up more sales with vast profit margins (admittedly for the manufacturers, rather than them) to fuel the next corporate contract, this shirt starts conversations. Not only about why a 55-year-old is still wearing football shirts (a fair point) but also from curious onlookers eager to find out more about a superb design showcasing values that have driven a

game-changing organisation to use the sport to impact the lives and health of millions of young people.

The results have been stunning, including reducing the incidence of HIV in South Africa by 50 per cent, increasing the number of people in Zambia who know their HIV status by 75 per cent and reducing the number of people in Zimbabwe who marry before the age of 18 by 25 per cent. And they are not resting on their laurels. They are developing new technologies to help them reach more young people with their health messages, including mobile apps, online platforms and interactive games. They are also collaborating with other organisations to amplify their effectiveness. Making the world a safer place for young people fuelled by buying a superbly stylish shirt. What's not to like?

8

Geoff's Story

SO THE saying 'Mind Always Matters' may just be one of many phrases people trot out without really paying much attention to it. Not so for me, as I will explain below. However, what has that got to do with football shirts? After all, to many non-football fans, football shirts are just overpriced lycra often worn too tightly by overweight middle-aged men!

There, I've said it, but hopefully that's got your attention.

Yes, football shirts could be considered by some as I've described above. However, to many, they offer a way to show which team you support and perhaps display your identity. Why else would so many wear their shirts when away on foreign holidays?

I am a football supporter. I support Hull City and have done since I was a young boy of around six when, like many youngsters, my dad took me to Boothferry Park. I distinguish between supporter and a fan as I 'support' my team, I attend matches home and away when I can and for years I've always followed my club, even from afar when working and living away from my hometown, trying to build a career, bringing up three small children when finances often prohibited attending games.

'Fans', for me, enjoy football, they follow many clubs, and may support one, possibly two. I've never fully understood the 'XYZ are my second club' argument by the way. The fans to whom I refer rarely attend matches, but with modern-day football finances these are the fans who pay their cash to TV companies who control, many feel ruin, football with the obscene amounts of cash that our game at the top level enjoys.

Having got that off my chest, where do the football shirts come in – in this contribution as 'Mind Always Matters', I and my colleagues at Hull City Supporters' Trust (HCST) managed to combine the two. Before I get there, please stay with me, as by way of an explanation for my motivation I will also share a personal aspect which has shaped me and my actions since August 2016.

In March 2016 I was elected as chairman of Hull City Supporters' Trust. I had been a director since it was re-launched in January 2015. The HCST entity is actually the Tigers Cooperative, an early supporters' trust established in December 1999 when Hull City were once again in dire straits and almost dropped out of the Football League but for a heroic recovery which in these parts has become known as 'the Great Escape'.

So I'm leading a well-known supporters' trust, well-known as it grew out of the successful campaign by a collaboration of Hull City fans' groups and fanzines called 'City 'Til We Die' to prevent the then owners changing the club's playing name to Hull Tigers. In 2016 Hull City were in the news again as the same owners abolished all concession pricing, reducing adult ticket prices too to be fair, but also forcing kids and OAPs to pay full adult prices. We were promoted back to the Premier League when we beat Sheffield Wednesday in the 2016 Championship play-off final at Wembley.

My own personal aspect came in August 2016, on the eve of the opening day of the new season when we kicked off the campaign playing then PL champions Leicester in a lunchtime fixture.

I was booked to do several media interviews on Friday, 12 August but midway through a Sky Sports interview with Rob Palmer, a Hull lad originally, one of my sons attempted suicide. That was out of the blue and totally unexpected. Life-changing events followed with his partial recovery over 11 months in the care of our wonderful NHS but the experiences of those months led me to do what I could to support suicide prevention, and crucially make attempts to remove the stigma, particularly men have, about discussing mental health issues. I was shocked to learn that 75 per cent of suicides are men: more shocked still that 12 men a day die by suicide.

Now, this is where football shirts come into play, as a couple of years later HCST were approached by a replica football shirts manufacturer, offering a kickback for each shirt sold. We looked at our historic kits, things of beauty for some but for others there were some real horrors. We asked if the company could replicate the iconic, for Hull City fans, 1992/93 tiger-striped shirt.

Now that was a shirt but one which at the time the club didn't sell many of.

We approached Hull City to ask if we could reproduce the club crest as, after several years of protesting against the then owners over their daft name-change idea, then campaigning to restore concessions, let's just say the owners and I didn't always agree on everything. They'd actively sought to remove me as HCST chairman throughout 2018, but failed, so it was a long shot. We were refused permission, due to copyright issues apparently, but it was expected so we settled for the HCST logo as a crest instead.

I did manage to get the approval from Sean Boanas, CEO of local electrical supplier, Bonus, to use their logo as shirt sponsor. That made our replica, well, homage really, more realistic as Bonus were shirt sponsors at Hull City for several years but we were then left to decide what to do with the sleeves.

I had the idea of adding two local charities. East Riding Dementia Friends and a men's mental health charity I was involved with, MindHealth, which ran weekly men's and women's chat sessions in Hull and East Yorkshire under the banners #BlokesUnited and #WomenUnited.

Our idea was to sell the shirts and donate profits made to the two charities who HCST were promoting on the shirt sleeves. We didn't expect to sell many shirts without the correct club logo, but I'm glad to say we were wrong.

The final sales of the charity tiger-striped shirt blew us away as we sold over 260! That enabled HCST to donate over £2,000 to local charities, with donations still to be made from the remaining funds received.

When we first thought of the idea the shirt production company offered to provide a couple of promotional shirts. We had one badged up with Windass 9 on the back. Deano is a local lad and a hero to many City fans. He was a young star who wore the 1992/93 shirt in question, but he's much better known for scoring the goal that promoted Hull to the Premier League for the first time in our history in May 2008. That goal sealed a massive turnaround in fortunes considering the club almost dropped out of the league in the late 90s. What a decade that was on reflection.

Dean was good enough to sign our promotional shirt recently when HCST arranged a signing session for his recently published book. We auctioned it off in 2023 to celebrate 15 years since he scored that goal at Wembley.

So there you have it. Football shirts can be a thing of beauty for some but they can also be a vehicle for good. I have to admit I am quite proud we have over 260 shirts which are worn at matches and events, displaying logos of worthy local charities advertising the great work they do. I know the charities in question appreciated the cash HCST donated so it was a win-win all round as far as I'm concerned.

So Mind Always Matters and combined with the idea of producing some charity-focussed replica Hull City shirts I am delighted to say the combined efforts of everyone involved who bought the shirts will result in over £3,000 being donated to the two charities involved together with Dovehouse Hospice in Hull benefitting too.

Geoff Bielby
Director and former chairman
Hull City Supporters' Trust

9

Uncomfortable Shirts

QATAR AND the fight for human rights – hope is not a strategy.

On 13 March 2023, FIFA officials were handed a petition organised by Amnesty and Avaaz (a US-based non-profit organisation promoting global activism) signed by over a million people demanding long-overdue justice for the migrant workers who toiled to create the Qatar 2022 World Cup stadiums. According to *The Guardian*, more than 6,500 migrant workers had died in the country over the previous decade with many of these deaths still not investigated. However, FIFA said that just 37 people had died in connection with the construction of the World Cup stadiums. Adding heft to the message was a specially designed shirt that was also handed to FIFA that brought the sordid story to life by using the blue and yellow workwear migrant workers wore in those brain-meltingly hot conditions. The back of the shirt had 'Justice 4 workers' with an unequivocal message on the left sleeve of 'Pay Up FIFA'.

Steve Cockburn, Amnesty International's head of economic and social justice, said, 'By presenting the football shirts at the FIFA Museum in Zürich we are demanding that the organisation recognises the sacrifice of migrant workers, and that their outstanding demands for compensation are met.'

The petition was financed by football shirts designed by Dublin-based creative agency Hen's Teeth the previous November. Their 'Goalissimo' range was made up of 13 funky and strident designs produced in the UK by manufacturers Vulfco. They went on sale just in time for Christmas on the Hen's Teeth website.

Four months earlier, as we gagged on the latest saccharine media spin for each World Cup kit, Denmark's designers Hummel made a bold and breathtaking statement on the motivation behind their design. They wanted to hark back to the Danes' hugely successful Euro '92 tournament but, more importantly, to 'protest against Qatar and its human rights record', a comment that would have Qatari apologist David Beckham spinning in his gold-plated jacuzzi. With this aim in mind, they chose to tone down all the design elements including their logo and the iconic chevrons as an act of quiet reflection for all the lives so needlessly lost in and around stadium construction and its surrounding infrastructure. This decision was profoundly underscored by a statement of piercing clarity, 'We don't wish to be visible during a tournament that has cost thousands of people their lives. We support the Danish national team all the way, but that isn't the same as supporting Qatar as a host nation.'

But Hummel, a Danish company that has a Premier League profile with Everton and ten clubs in the Championship for the 2023/24 season, has gone further than a token tournament gesture with one kit. All three options carry the same philosophy, particularly the black version that, in 'the colour of mourning', honours all the fallen expat workers in the carnival of hubris, and the first kit, described by them as being 'blood red'. To give tangible support for Amnesty International's work on human rights, the manufacturers also gave part (a measly one per cent, it has to be said) of each shirt sale to fund their spotlighting of heartbreaking violations of human dignity across the globe. Although there has been some criticism that these sentiments weren't openly expressed when the original kit was launched, it honours a promise made by the Danish FA in November 2021 to play with 'critical messages' on their kits. They had considered adding a black armband to the standard design but felt this would put players in a difficult situation (shown by the FIFA veto of England's One Love captain's armband). Another strategy rejected was to put messages about human rights in the fabric and, as a last resort, to abandon designing their national kit entirely.

As night follows day, there was predictable online outrage at Hummel's 'virtue signalling' and 'gaslighting' that trotted out the same tedious tropes thrown at anyone raising their head above the antisocial media barricade. Having said that, Hummel has designed kits for a Qatar Stars League team in the past, a group of a dozen clubs that German company Puma supplies over half of the league's apparel to without feeling squeamish about what they are attaching their brand to. Indeed, for the 2023/24 season, Hummel were happy to take the piles of Qatari Riyal to design the kits of Al-Rayyan, Al-Ahli and Al Sadd without having their conscience pricked.

The Qataris weren't overpleased at their World Cup party being pooped, either. Their Pythonesque (look it up, kids) sounding Qatar Supreme Committee (as opposed to the Supreme Committee of Qatar and those splitters at the Qatar Committee of the Supreme) accused Hummel of 'trivialising' the country's 'genuine commitment' to worker safety. In a breathtaking display of whataboutery, they went on to accuse the rest of the world, especially the home of Peter Schmeichel, of failing to do more to protect human rights, levelling this charge, 'The onus should always be on countries to do more to protect the rights of peoples all over the world, including in Denmark.'

This would be the Denmark that comes out annually in the Champions League of places for standards of living, quality of education, universal healthcare, low crime rates and family-friendly government policies. A brave target to aim for, Qatar.

It's always good to get the perspective of the 'Sultan of Shirts', Phil Delves, head of content at Football Shirt Collective. For him, Hummel's stand, rather than being a one-off piece of guerrilla marketing, is the start of a more values-driven approach to football shirt design. But, focussing on Denmark's stance, the timing of their comments was one issue for Phil, 'Hummel's timing of the protest statement seemingly flew in the face of the initial press release that accompanied the kit launch. Go back and you'll see no mention at all of Qatar in the marketing. Was this a stunt from Hummel designed to drum up excitement and sales after a lacklustre launch week?'

Phil doesn't see this as a stunt. For him, it has much more resonance with the values of the team, country and manufacturer. It would also have been a big distraction with the Danes about to play the final game of their Nations League campaign after the launch. Phil also doesn't buy into the conspiracy theory that this was a stance borne of poor initial shirt sales, 'The suggestion that the statement was in response to an underwhelming reaction to the shirt is also far-fetched in my eyes. It's true that the shirt was received with largely mixed to negative reviews within the shirt community, but that's not necessarily indicative of the overall response. Monochrome shirts are typically quite popular with the general public (there's a reason that blackout shirts have been all the rage), and the shirt community bubble is just that, a bubble which can act like an echo chamber at times. Add to that the fact that it would be too early to properly gauge sales, and this again looks like a planned stunt.'

Phil is intrigued that, with all the other options available to the players, team, country and Hummel, they chose to use their kit to drive their point home by cleverly pre-empting FIFA's rage at undermining their paymaster's reputation while clearly showing their discomfort at being associated with a tournament built on the bodies of dead migrant workers. FIFA has been elegantly hamstrung by Hummel. They need to be seen to act to prevent further outbreaks of compassion and protect their monetised mouthpieces like David Beckham and Gary Neville, but this will further add a profile to Hummel's cause while doing nothing comes with similar risks. Unfortunately, Denmark gave more ammunition to ridicule rather than admiration on the pitch. Their early exit after finishing third in Group D thanks to a single win over Tunisia will have made for jovial conversations in Qatari VVIP boxes.

Qatar doesn't hold a monopoly on uncomfortable shirts. Arsenal's invitation for us to 'Visit Rwanda' preceded former heartless home secretaries Priti Patel and Suella Braverman's plans to forcibly relocate asylum seekers there, but it remained a deeply divisive decision by the Gooners. For three seasons starting in 2018 and then, despite loud criticism, renewed in 2021, they have played with the sleeve sponsorship, which also saw the Rwandan flag flown at Arsenal's Emirates Stadium. This deal annually transferred a cool £30m from the cash-strapped country (via their tourism board for plausible deniability) to the north London millionaires who chose this agreement as the first time they agreed to have sleeve sponsors. At least the bar is set low for the next partner. To be fair, Paris Saint-Germain have also dipped into the impoverished Central African coffers with their women's team and stadium promoting the delights of the country for a reported £10m for a three-year deal. With the Rwandan government accused by a range of human rights groups (including the highly respected Human

Rights Watch) of regular torture and extra-judicial killings, this seems a deeply problematic partnership for a league that can surely cherry-pick the very best of brands that are transparent and ethical, if only it conducted the simplest of due diligence.

Arsenal were forced to accept that the Rwanda partnership had become more uncomfortable after the UK asylum deal, although it could be argued that it shone a harsher light on the British government than that of Rwanda. It also spoke to the insane inflationary spiral of English football's massive overspending on wages that makes club budgets more unsustainable with every passing season as they fend off increasing demands from fans for big names on wages equivalent to the GDP of small countries. This tempts them to park principles at the stadium gates and focus more on due dollars than diligence. Talking of which, Rwanda, one of the world's 20 poorest countries, with a GDP per capita of around US$1,000 in 2022 (and heavily reliant on foreign aid to pay its bills) has transferred tens of millions to a glamorous British football club sitting in a country whose GDP per capita stood at US$45,500 for the same year.

But over and above the money, there is the heartbreaking thought that this is just an exercise in sports washing for the Rwandan regime to sanitise their actions and force western clubs to legitimise them through association. Ultimately, government spin doctors sitting in the glistening capital city of Kigali while rural poverty runs rampant know that he who pays the piper plays the tune.

Shirts can also show how even an experienced, global brand can hire Donald Duck for due diligence. Note to Adidas: when designing World Cup apparel for a nation in a historically feisty relationship with one of its neighbours, check your workings before you launch. North Africa's Algeria and Morocco don't need any kindling to reignite a fire that's been burning for three-quarters of a century along their near 2,000km shared border. Instructively for the German designers, as recently as 2021 Algeria cut ties with its neighbour after accusing them of hostile acts, so this was a project that should have been labelled 'approach with extreme caution' rather than 'bang something out on a Friday afternoon that looks vaguely north African/ Arabic chic'.

When Algeria's World Cup design was launched in late September 2022, I would love to have seen the Adidas marketing team's faces as they reviewed the social media 'engagement'. From spin doctors to PR trauma paramedics in seconds. Morocco was not happy. They felt this shirt was a piece of cultural appropriation where their much larger southern neighbours had again taken what didn't belong to them. The designers had tried to celebrate the geometric designs of the El Mechouar Palace in Algeria but, to Moroccans quick to choler, their choice was part of a *Zellige* (a form of Islamic art) design common to many Moroccan mosaics. Moving the battleground from disputing who owned Western Sahara to footballers' bodies, the Moroccan Ministry of Culture even went as far as issuing legal papers to Adidas.

It's astonishing that, as part of the process, the manufacturers didn't factor in the worst-case scenario and concept-test their work from both sides of the barricades when approaching kits for such a volatile region. Somewhere in the Adidas organisation, there's someone specialising in making coffee that used to be a shirt designer.

Maybe they should have opted for the soft shoe approach of Jeremy Clarkson in his Netflix documentary, *Clarkson's Farm 2*. Determined to win over the hearts and minds of the local village consistently, through their town council, rejecting every Diddly Squat Farm initiative, he thought that sponsoring the shirt of the local football team, Chadlington FC, in 2021 would unfreeze some of the councillors' icy hearts. The Witney and District FA club were quick to make the most of their Netflix moment in the sun and in February 2023 sold the shirts on their website. The Umbro-designed tops went for only £25, which was a great way to spread the word of the club across the globe, sold out almost immediately and included a magnificent golden rampant lion crest for these pub league players. Hearing about it, the *Daily Mail* reported this project as running parallel to Ryan Reynolds taking over Wrexham FC earlier that year. Desperate to come up with an 'angle', the sponsorship of two dozen odd village team jerseys was breathlessly reported as, 'It makes Clarkson the latest celebrity to invest in football clubs, after Hollywood stars Ryan Reynolds and Rob McElhenney took over Wrexham FC earlier this year.'

That must have been the slowest of news days.

10

Football Shirts For Charity

THERE WAS a touching circularity for Football Shirts For Charity when Chris Berry decided in late 2022 to raise funds for Prostate Cancer UK by walking 26 miles between the stadiums of Portsmouth and Southampton carrying 26 football shirts. When the journey was complete, he gave a selection of them to Tania Harding and Jayme Sporton to make the kits work even harder for great causes.

I met Tania and Jayme on 30 August 2022 when, before they were received as VIP guests at Exeter City before playing Newport County, they met my wife and I for a drink and chat. We were bowled over by their passion and drive. We knew immediately that their campaign would resonate with everyone they came across. The day before, the Grecians had become winners of the Football Shirts Charity 5k competition for the third time in a row, which had raised money for the Bobby Moore Fund and a Ukrainian humanitarian charity. Now let me hand you over to the experts.

Tania and Jayme wrote, 'Football is the national sport and transcends all generations and all walks of life. If you're reading this, as we all know, it is a very special community that provides belonging and togetherness. As massive football fanatics and having both been affected by cancer in people very close to us, we saw an opportunity to do something about it. We wanted to do something different. We established Football Shirts For Charity.

'We are the UK's only charity organisation dedicated exclusively to selling retro, pre-loved, vintage and sometimes new football shirts from all over the world whether it be from the Premier League, the EFL, international teams, or non-league football teams from across the globe for example. Our strapline is that "Every Shirt Has A Story".

'The sight of any football shirt always evokes so many special memories and conversations. Football Shirts For Charity was born from the love of knowing the pride in securing ownership of a pre-loved, historic, retro or vintage football shirt, while also contributing to vital charities. Our online shop is the chance to secure ownership of a retro, historic, recent, pre-loved or vintage football shirt at the same time as contributing to vital charities. We pride ourselves in trying hard to feature a really wide range of shirts from international and the Premier League, right down to local and lower-pyramid non-league football – and similarly, we try to have shirts that can cater for all budgets.

'The profit from all sales goes 100 per cent to charity. Our current main charities are the Bobby Moore Fund and Cancer Research UK.

'The future success of our organisation obviously depends on our capacity to secure football shirts and associated kit from incredibly generous donations. If somebody has a spare shirt they no longer wear and are in a position to donate it to us, this can be put to very good use. Shirts can be sent to us directly, or we can collect them if we can. People can use the contact form on our website for an address, or to discuss anything else for that matter. We really love to engage with the football community – and hear other people's great stories and ideas.

'We have also released our very own FSFC football shirts which can be seen in the photos attached – and these are available to buy on our website. The main panel with the manufacturer badge and FSFC logo is the only black panel. We wanted there to be a fading of grey so that every panel below gets slightly lighter. The pattern on the sleeve gives it a distinct style, adding a feature to the shirt while blending in with the shirt's main grey panels. The accent colours in blue, amber and red fade across the shirt in opposite directions which makes the colour pop against the background grey-black colours. The accent colours also feature subtly on the collar and sleeve cuffs. The stunning name and number set

are available for free in the matching accent colour. "One Shirt. Three Choices. You Decide" emerged as a natural strapline to help showcase this unique buying opportunity. #EveryShirtHasAStory

'Football Shirts For Charity also holds several events throughout the year for literally anybody to become proactively involved, such as the Football Shirt Charity 5k that has just entered its third year and third season.

This is a very exciting virtual event where you can join us by running, walking, cycling or swimming five kilometres, any time, anywhere, to raise money for our nominated charities. For a £10 entry fee, you will not only receive one of our unique Football Shirt Charity 5k medals, but the event will also contribute to our league table. Each entry scores a point for the entrant's nominated football club – and this can be literally ANY club. These events can also be found on our website.

'In the last three months of 2022, we were fortunate enough to have a three-month pop-up retail space at the Festival Place shopping centre in Basingstoke, Hampshire. This was an incredible experience and opportunity for our organisation and in just 50 trading days, we were able to donate well in excess of £9,000 to the Bobby Moore Fund and Cancer Research UK via shop floor sales. The sight of football shirts on the shop floor really did evoke so many special memories and conversations with such a vast and eclectic mix of customers, which was such an important, exciting and valuable aspect of this project, in addition to raising such a large amount of money. We're very keen on having the opportunity to make this an annual event and returned again in November 2023.

'To summarise, the best way people could support us is by donating football shirts they no longer want, buying shirts from our online shop and/or by entering an event like the Football Shirt Charity 5k and supporting whichever team they choose to support. We love interacting with the football and football shirt kit community. We're on Twitter (@fsfcUK), Instagram (football.shirts.fc) and Facebook, but the best place to find us is probably at our website, www. footballshirtsfc.co.uk.

'If you are in a position to donate us even one football shirt, that would be truly amazing. We're happy to collect shirts if we can and from any level of the football pyramid. Just please get in touch. We absolutely love what we do. We are currently a small organisation, but have very, very big dreams and we would like to thank you for helping Football Shirts For Charity to make a difference. Please feel free to contact us if you think you can help in any way whatsoever. Thank you for taking the time to read this and for helping Football Shirts For Charity to make a difference. Further information, details about the charities we currently support, our events and our shop can be found at our website.'

* * *

Continuing to make a lasting difference

2023 saw the dynamic duo achieve remarkable milestones in their mission to make a positive impact. Through the sale of football shirts and the generous support of their community, they successfully raised over £9,000 for the two charities.

April 2023: a 5k run

Tania and Jayme organised a charity 5K run in April 2023, which attracted an impressive turnout of over 100 participants. The event not only promoted a healthy and active lifestyle but also raised over £1,000 for the

Bobby Moore Fund and Sebastian's Action Trust. It exemplified the football shirt community's willingness to support charitable causes through engaging in sporting activities.

May 2023: uniting through a charity match

In May 2023, Football Shirts For Charity partnered with a local football club to host a charity match. The event attracted a crowd of over 200 people and proved to be a resounding success, raising more than £500 for the two charities. The match highlighted the unifying power of sports, bringing people together for a noble cause.

June 2023: summer of giving

Looking ahead, Football Shirts For Charity announced plans to organise a series of fundraising events throughout the summer. These events included a football tournament, a bake sale, and a raffle. By offering various opportunities for individuals to contribute and support the charities, they aim to further their impact and reach.

11

Rock 'n' Roll Football Shirts

FOOTBALL AND music form the perfect partnership. Both passions invite us to (sometimes ridiculous) flights of fancy and seemingly limitless indulgence when nothing else in our lives receives such a free pass.

Credit Tony Kirk

When I was a student in Manchester I decided to cement my love of Kate Bush's music by joining her fan club. I met up with other group members in one of their houses and saw a framed photo of a Ceefax page (look it up, kids) that mentioned her in passing. I realised I had been splashing in the fandom toddler pool and accidentally plunged into the Olympic tryouts of music obsessives. But football and music are the broadest of churches. A passing interest can lead to enjoyable diversion, but can also head you down ever-increasing rabbit holes of glorious geekery and, unlike a crypto bro persuading us to 'buy the dip' of 80 per cent, music and football create very few casualties – shirt collectors being defined as 'harmless' seems to embed a passive aggressive undercurrent – and allows us to recreate our pasts with sound and occasional fury (looking at you, Napalm Death) that signifies something personal to us.

Both pursuits also demand a high degree of loyalty. I try to explain to my students at work that loyalty doesn't only mean you carry on buying the goods or service over time, but you continue to do so even when there is a better offer. Even after decades of having your eardrums pleasantly shredded by Napalm Death, you continue to mosh to their brand of caterwauling rather than take a more risk-off approach with something that doesn't peel paint from your walls, even if you know growling to 'Unchallenged Hate' in your middle age doesn't go down well with the neighbours in the local railway club bar. Loyalty is a beguiling calling card to isolate you from those judging this as regressive posturing and create an attractive catalyst for people who warm to the ideals of lowering our social defences to find a common cause. Or, as someone once said, 'At the end of the day, I'd rather be excluded for who I include, than be included for who I exclude.'

Credit Tony Kirk

This brings me back to the delights of Rock 'n' Roll Football Shirts. I mentioned them in my first book's chapter on musical kits (thank you if you bought it) but soon felt the need to dive in deeper. After forming the business in 2019, Dan Hinksman oversaw a nascent firm with an innovative and quirky approach before being battered into existential crisis by the horrific headwinds of our first pandemic lockdown of the following year. As he shared when interviewed by the *i* in July 2022, his business, like a rock band or Oldham Athletic, had the chance to hit the high notes, almost disappeared entirely and is now determined to rise again.

He explained, 'You have to just put it to the back of your mind and just go "look, these are the cards you have been dealt, you just have to play it the best you can". But it does get to you.'

Scrolling through the catalogue, shirts target my expanding girth demographic by offering sizes up to XXL. As someone living in Manchester during the 'Madchester' years, bands celebrated through their shirts resonate with the memories of Factory Records including Joy Division's *Unknown Pleasures*, and a healthy showing for more of Manchester's own with shirts featuring the Stone Roses and James. Designs also riff on national shirts with a Wales-style top replacing

Credit Tony Kirk

the badge with a two-fingered salute and phrase of 'man don't give a f***', while the Scotland-style shirt declares that they are, like Primal Scream from their *Screamadelica* album, 'Movin' On Up'.

Embedded in Dan's ethos is a mission statement that drives him:

'Love the music

Love the game

Stand out from the crowd.'

Like so many other examples in this book, Dan explores the bravery of simply standing away from the crowd and, when bad news buffets him, he determines to keep going and refuses to buckle or compromise. The wonderful thing about standing your ground for what you believe in is that, sometimes, the rest of the world thinks you might be on to something. A brand tired and trying to remain relevant, in August 2022 Admiral released two shirts that riffed on their own iconic designs to showcase the Jam and the Style Council. The remake of the England 1982 shirt focusses on the Jam as this was the year they split up and references their fan club badge on the shirt and one of their concert tickets on the tag. For the Style Council shirt, Admiral focus on their iconic 1970s silhouettes with logos repeated down a raised sleeve tape, and 'Internationalists' is used on the front to celebrate the band's Live Aid performance in 1985. Only 300 of these shirts were produced, with each one being numbered on the front.

I spoke to Dan in late 2022 and asked him why he does what he does. He replied, 'It's definitely a labour of love. I've spent a lot of time, effort and money for (so far) very little financial reward. I've been constantly advised or asked why I don't provide the standard customised T-shirt service. The honest answer is, because doing something that is mundane to me doesn't provide the motivation I require to bring out the best in me and scratch the creative itch that I have a deep rooted passion for. Also, creating and producing a fresh and alternative product to the traditional band shirt, is far more fulfilling on a personal level.'

I then asked about what originally inspired him, 'For as long as I can remember, I've always had a keen interest in football shirts. Several years ago, I became aware of an Adidas skateboarding brand concept/product in which Adidas collaborated with other traditional skateboard brands to create alternative football shirt designs. I immediately thought these were extremely interesting and very cool. This planted a seed that lay dormant for a couple of years until I was watching the 2018 World Cup. Riding the crest of a euphoric wave of England's unexpected progress to the latter stages of the competition, I had the lightbulb moment of marrying music and football in the form of football shirts.'

On the design process, Dan spoke of how he came about initial ideas, 'Inspiration can be born from either an existing kit of a club/country's (current or previous) shirt design or something as simple as listening to a song on the radio or from my personal collection. However, the example I'm going to use here was actually conceived from a suggestion by an Instagram follower. The concept was a non-club-affiliated "Madchester" shirt. I was immediately drawn to the song "24 Hour

Party People" by Happy Mondays along with the iconic Hacienda nightclub and the city's industrial history. At this point, these are just ideas in my head. With regard to a specific existing shirt, the Manchester City 2019/20 away shirt dominated my initial thoughts with its obvious nod to the Hacienda. Using a 2D template to piece together the design – I use a basic 2D template to bring various design ideas together in order to visualise the shirt (torso front/back, collar and sleeves) – I start with the basics: base colour, sleeve style/colour; addition of stripes? For this design I decided to centralise the yellow diagonal hazard tape stripes as a focal point of the torso. This would be overlayed on to a deep charcoal/ smoke grey base colour.'

When it comes to adding background detail, Dan continued, 'This is the area where I decided to use a

Credit Tony Kirk

strong industrial influence. Having previously worked in the manufacturing industry, I used my experience of being exposed to factory environments to choose an appropriate repeating pattern which would synergise with the overall "feel" of the shirt design. To do this I chose to apply an industrial checker plate flooring pattern to the background of the charcoal/smoke grey base colour. I start by taking a photographic image and 'tracing' it using computer software to create a basic vector. This is then superimposed over the background colour.

Credit Tony Kirk

Dan also spoke of the essential design elements on each shirt, 'There's always essential aspects that feature on every shirt design I produce which give them the unmistakable football shirt look. These include: sponsor text/logo (usually a song or album title); a badge/crest; name and number on the back of the jersey. For this shirt design I had already decided, from the initial thought process, that the "sponsor" text would be the song title/slogan "24 Hour Party People" as this epitomised the party culture of the "Madchester" era of the city. I also wanted to incorporate the worker bee (the official symbol of Manchester) as well as a basic factory silhouette and phrase "Mad Fer It" into the shirt badge/ crest. The last major addition is the name and number that adorns the back of the jersey. For this design the choice was obvious: Ryder (Shaun Ryder) and 87 (1987, the year the song was released). I added the hazard/ chevron lines to the number to give it a unique look and add some extra detail.'

Once Dan's shirt design is complete, he submits it to the manufacturer along with the relevant Pantone colour references and alignment instructions, ready for production.

He says that receiving manufactured shirts is the most rewarding part of the whole process, 'What was once just a basic idea in your head becoming something you can physically hold/wear/see with your own eyes is so satisfying and makes, what can sometimes be a process taking months to come to fruition, worth all the effort.'

I then spoke to Dan in early 2023 to find out more about his values and inspiration.

Matt:
'What are some of the things you have learned about yourself over this highly challenging start to your business buffeted by Covid and a cost of living crisis?'

Dan:
'I learned that I can't do EVERYTHING myself and to accept the kind offers of help from others. I've realised

Credit Tony Kirk

that I'm pretty good at problem solving and (as much as I hate to) I'm reasonably good at making compromises. Also, to trust my judgement and stay true to what I believe to be the best course of action.'

Matt:

'Who were some of your strongest allies in the early days of your business?'

Dan:

'My wife Jude has been my biggest supporter, making personal sacrifices in order for me to pursue my dream as well as providing financial support during the difficult Covid times. My cousin Phil (who is also my closest friend) has been invaluable when it comes to discussing my ideas as well as giving constructive feedback and moral support. Outside support has come from local football teams Rossendale Valley Stags Junior Football Club and Rimington Football Club, both welcoming my small business into the football community with open arms. I'd also like to thank the Clone Roses for offering me the priceless experience of trading at their Spike Island 30th anniversary celebration of the iconic Stone Roses performance during the second Covid summer of 2021.'

Matt:
'What advice would you give someone wanting to create a business similar to yours?'

Dan:
'My advice would be to have a LOT of patience and maintain a strong belief in yourself. Reach out to others if you need help but also develop a thick skin – there are a number of spiteful idiots out there (especially on social media) that seem to take pleasure in rubbishing your work. Ignore them or use them as motivation to succeed. It's also worth noting that for every idiot on social media, there's at least five people offering help and support.'

Matt:
'What's one thing you wish you had known when you began?'

Dan:
'I wish I'd known just how long it can take to establish yourself as a relatively niche product. Take small steps –

it's a learning curve, so take your time and spend/invest your money wisely.'

Matt:

'Did you have any "a-ha!" moments that made you rethink your approach?'

Dan:

'I've realised that, as much as you believe in yourself, always "test the waters" before making financial commitments – I still have some stock of the shirts I made for the launch of the business over three years ago. As a result, I only produce a limited amount of stock for new designs.'

Matt:

'Can you pick out the top three things you are most proud of as you look back on the life of your business?'

Dan:

'One, actually getting the company/brand up and running without any previous business experience. Two, teaching myself how to develop achievable shirt designs from scratch using design software I'd never worked with before. Three, my actual designs, especially the latest ones from the last 12 months, I'm extremely proud of.'

Matt:

'If you could choose only one of your shirts to own, which one would it be and why?'

Dan:

'If I could choose one of my shirts to own, it would be a variation of an existing design that I've not actually released. It's a Celtic (green and white hoops) version of the "MOVIN' ON UP" shirt. Although I have no footballing or cultural allegiance to the club, I've always loved the Celtic home shirts and couldn't resist designing one with the obvious connection to Bobby Gillespie of Primal Scream.'

Matt:

'Do you have any issues with copyright from the big kit producers?'

Dan:

'No, I've had no issues there. My philosophy to shirt design has always been inspiration rather than imitation.'

Matt:

'Are there clubs that you would not partner with as they don't share your values?'

Dan:

'I cannot think of any clubs off the top of my head that I wouldn't partner with. Although, a couple of years ago I did approach a local professional club (that I'll choose not to name) with which I have family connections and suggested a collaboration which would prove mutually beneficial on a PR front. However, this club's response was very disappointing as they only seemed to be interested in trying to obtain money from me (and at the time I most certainly didn't have any!).'

Matt:

'Looking ahead, how do you see your business evolving?'

Dan:

'In the immediate future, I'll be taking my products to sell at an increasing number of live music events. Looking further ahead I see my business evolving by introducing a children's range of shirt designs. I'd also like to dip my toe in different genres of music such as hip hop (possibly as an NFL or NBA-style jersey or vest).'

12

Cross Stitch Shirts

I'M CONSTANTLY inspired by people who pursue their passion projects irrespective of the putrid opinions of the Twitterati. In my last book (if I can't plug myself, then who can?) I reflected on my six years working in Thai football.

Its title sums up my experiences. *Thai Football Tales: a Beautiful Madness* looks back on my decision to abandon a perfectly lucrative career to dive headlong into the niche world of Thai football, then explore a smaller niche of English media and then, for a niche to the power of three, to become an English media officer for local clubs. But, as Dave Murray of Cross Stitch Shirts shows, there is something profoundly freeing about following a path much less travelled. In the interests of full disclosure, Dave has made two gorgeous creations based on the shirts I designed to promote the first *Kit and Caboodle* shirt, and they overlook my work desk as I type this.

If you think this is the way to curry my favour, then you are probably right.

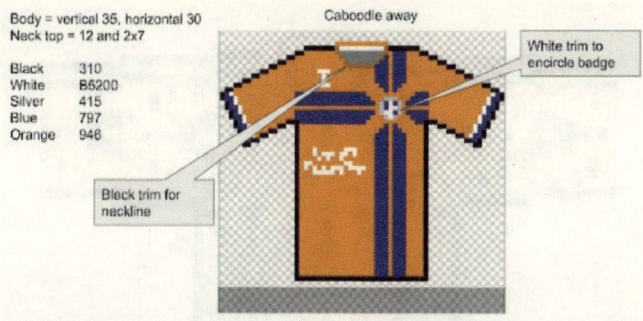

Body = vertical 35, horizontal 30
Neck top = 12 and 2x7

Black   310
White   B5200
Silver   415
Blue   797
Orange   948

Caboodle away

White trim to
encircle badge

Black trim for
neckline

I spoke to Dave in late 2022 to get his perspective and, more importantly, find out more about his drive and what he gets back from his creations.

Matt:

'Why do anything?'

Dave:

'I felt like I needed to do something different to avoid just doom-scrolling in front of the telly, something

139

that would produce a tangible output, that would show progress and balance a challenge and something automatic. My wife knits and produces the most amazing scarves, shawls and socks, so I suppose I was already leaning towards something "crafty".'

Matt:

'So why cross-stitch?'

Dave:

'There was no single trigger, but rather a series of little things that all came together. I'd tried knitting – I can do anything you like as long as it's rectangular. I'd tried crochet – that was just frustrating. I remembered making cross-stitch patterns at infant school. I remembered playing the classic *Sensible Soccer* games from when I was (much) younger and loved their art style. I'd seen the fabulous pictures produced by @8BitFootball and they just sort of appealed to me. And lastly, I bought a new tablet which came with a free pixel art drawing package. From all of that, the idea developed, so I bought a kit to give it a go (obviously, as a Leicester City fan, I went for one with a fox) and found it to be relaxing and interesting, yet something I could do and still engage with the world.

'However, the commercial kits I found were all a bit twee, so having realised that there was effectively an infinite range of football kits and with a sudden burst of confidence of "well how hard can it be?" I produced a design and jumped right in. From that starting point, I've found a hobby that has connected me with people across the world. It also gives me puzzles to solve and keeps me engaged, from the initial plan for the shirt, through to how to best present the finished piece.'

Matt:

'What is the right colour/tone/hue/contrast?'

Dave:

'How can I represent the design with the constraints of pixels/scale/detail so it doesn't look blocky?

Representing text is the trickiest, trying to balance the correct impression with what is possible. What is the most efficient route for the stitches for time and thread (and avoiding complications at the edge of the frame)?'

Dave then spoke about the stages he goes through, using the *Kit and Caboodle* away shirt as an example:

Plan

'This is not (and doesn't pretend to be) a "proper" cross-stitch pattern, but it works for me, so it's what I use. The hatched background is from the drawing package I use and allows me to count the required stitches. The dark grey hatched area is movable and scaled to the same pitch as the main picture. It is effectively a stitch guide that allows me to count the stitches in an individual row and then move it down, one row at a time so I don't lose track. The notes in the top right are to help with the overall scale and list the thread colours I need for the pattern. The call-outs are for additional specific information that I can't show in the basic picture, but add detail to the finished shirt.'

Equipment

'The threads, as per the plan, and the fabric hoop are the key parts, with the little fox (LCFC hint again) needle minder (two magnets that clip to the fabric and hold the needle when not in use) and the thread holder that uses some of my – possibly excessive – Lego to good effect.'

Ready to go

'I find stitching the border first gives me a reference to work from, for the other shirt elements (e.g. badge is x stitches in from the armpit).'

Colours

'The general rule is to stitch the dark colours first, but this is more of a guideline. This can also lead to some fun colour combinations as the shirt develops, in the case of *Kit and Caboodle*, something that looks a bit "Finland-esque".'

Trim

'Usually using backstitch and based on the call-outs on the plan, used to add detail/outline to key parts of the design. Shown to good effect on this shirt to highlight the badge and to provide definition for the neckline.'

Wash and iron

'To clean up the shirt and remove any grubby hand prints and rinse off any loose threads I've missed.'

Framing

'The final step for presentation uses a wooden frame to hold the shirt, replacing the frankly gaudy pink hoop that I use for the stitching.'

Dan also picked out five examples of kits showing the different techniques he has learned:

Basic stitch – Leicester City home, 1983/84

'My first shirt was always going to be a Leicester City one, so why not make it a copy of the first shirt I ever had, and in fact still do, now modelled on a teddy bear I made at school? This shirt uses the basic stitch, all in the same direction, working along the row from bottom

left to top right (//////) and then back again going bottom
right to top left (\\\\\\) to make the cross.'

Backstitch – Köln home, 2017/18

'This shirt added backstitch, which creates a thinner line between the standard stitches, often used for highlight/outline. In this case, I used different thicknesses of thread to recreate the blending between the dark and lighter red of the stripes.'

Half and half – Arsenal away, 1991–1993 (the 'Bruised Banana')

'To achieve the blend/fade between the dark blue and yellow, I used half and half stitches, where the cross is made up of stitches in two colours, one for each part. In this shirt, the colours are quite distinct, mirroring the effect on the actual design, but the technique also works for a more subtle blending where the colours are closer. The shirt also shows a good example of backstitch to

provide additional red trim on the sleeve stripes and to outline the sponsor text.'

Colour twist – Bradford City 2022/23

'A development of backstitch, but using two threads of different colours twisted together to produce a varied effect, such as a narrow trim on shirt cuffs or neck.'

French knots – Club Universitario de Deportes, special edition

'French knots are a technique that makes a small knot/ dot of thread, used here to rather good effect for the buttons on the placket.'

Outline – Pescara 2019/20, special edition

'I know this was a five-a-side, but I've decided to allow myself a "substitute" and include my version of the Pescara special edition (designed by Luigi D'Agostino and brought out to "give a kick to Covid-19"), which is frankly awesome and also, conveniently shows the use of backstitch to outline elements of the design as per the original.'

13

York City FC: History Resides In Us

ON 4 August 2022 Manchester City released a third kit that was yellow and black to the untrained eye. But think again. In reality, it 'celebrates Manchester creativity with a Fizzy Light and Parisian Night Colour palette'. As someone who lived in Manchester for three years, it beautifully evokes those golden sunsets setting over Whalley Range through the eternal drizzle. Far away from headily overpaid Premier League spin doctors sit York City FC in the National League. Celebrating their centenary, they decided to enlist the help of award-winning British designer Christopher Payne and, thanks to the help of the club's Kieran Archer, I had the pleasure of learning about how he made sure the first 100 years would be crowned by shirts of rare beauty and deep resonance.

Each kit elegantly spoke to the city's rich heritage and how its club reflected its values, including a highly evocative away kit. Chris's work created a yearning for the prelapsarian non-Premier League days with his 'chocolate and cream' away design for the 2022/23

season, celebrating the city's chocolate-making heritage in colours last worn in the 1930s. I'm grateful to Kieran, Chris and club photographer Tom Poole for sharing this uplifting story with me. But enough of my rambling. Let's hand over to Chris to walk us through his symphony of decisions and respectful, artistic and community-driven collaborations he oversaw. Are you reading carefully, Castore?

Chris explained, 'In 2022, I was brought in to design York City FC's historic centenary crest. Inspired by past

identities and conversations with passionate, lifelong York City FC supporters, this special edition crest was used to celebrate 100 years of York City Football Club.

'In addition to designing the centenary crest, I also designed a brand pattern that drew inspiration from York's famous Minster. This brand pattern was used on the football club's kits for the 2022/23 season. I looked at the shapes that made the Minster so unique and abstractly placed them together to form the kit's base pattern. If you look at the kit's design, you can see key York Minster features such as the Rose Window and the Five Sisters (among other recognisable features) woven into the design.

'In addition to the club's official centenary crest, I also designed a secondary identity that was used on select merchandise, marketing and business collateral throughout the centenary 2022/23 campaign.

'When a famous football club like York City reaches out to you, excitement is a normal reaction. But this was different. They were asking me to be part of an important landmark in the club's history. This is the story of how I joined forces with York City Football Club to create their centenary crest.

'Dan Simmonite is York City's media officer. He expertly runs the club's social media and digital marketing channels and is considered one of the best in the business. In fact, many aspiring sports marketers use his work as a benchmark. Dan became aware of my work in 2020 when I launched Eastleigh FC's new identity. This included a launch video titled *Chapters*. He was very complimentary about the project and got in touch to ask if I would appear on his podcast, *The Press Conference Pod*. I said yes immediately. We recorded a great chat that covered my design process, the impact of the launch, the design decisions that made Eastleigh Football Club's crest, and my overall experience in the world of football branding. A few months passed before Dan reached out again. This time, he had an idea and he wanted me to help execute it. He sent me a private message via Twitter:

'"Hey, Chris,

'"Next season will be York City's 100th anniversary and the club are thinking of introducing a special edition badge to commemorate this important moment in the club's history. We'd like to see if you would be interested in designing the club's centenary crest?"

'I said yes without hesitation, but the reality of this prestigious offer soon sank in. Designing a new identity for such a storied football club was a huge responsibility. I was confident I could do a great job for Dan and the club, and my initial excitement turned into

a determination to do the best job possible. I knew that this would be a great project to work on, with 99 years of history to draw inspiration from. My first instinct was to involve the passionate York City fans as much as possible.

'Dan and I met many times to discuss the project and the club. We both agreed that the fans should be heavily involved and that their voices should influence the design long before pen met paper. Dan used the club's media channels to announce that York City would be introducing a special centenary crest. In the same press release, he announced that I would be designing it and that we were looking for fans to share their thoughts. The announcement was typical of Dan's open and honest style, giving fans a clear picture of what was going on behind the scenes.

'While Dan was beginning the conversation with York City's supporters, I began my independent research into the club's history. My fact-finding mission covered the club's entire existence. Highs and lows. Club legends on and off the pitch. Cherished moments. Fascinating folklore. It was all there in spades. I soon learned that York City truly is a wonderful club with a captivating history, but the history books only tell one side of the story. It was time to learn from the people who live and dream in red, blue, and white.

'A vital part of our learning was encouraging supporters to share their experiences with us. Our first touchpoint was an online survey that allowed us to assess the sentiment for past identities, old kits, and moments in history. We sent out the survey to the club's large fan base, asking multiple questions. The results were fascinating.

'As the survey responses flooded in, Dan and I organised a series of focus groups with York City's fans. I designed a presentation that would help guide the conversations and help trigger memories that the fans were fond of. We invited the club's extremely knowledgeable and likeable historian, Paul Bowser, to join us. Paul helped us host the sessions. He was great at getting the conversation flowing and encouraging fans to freely air their views. The discussions we had were truly inspiring. We spoke for hours about everything from past players and famous games to favourite kits and club traditions. We also spoke in-depth about the club's previous identities. I learned a lot and became more and more enamoured with York City Football Club.

'The starting point for the centenary crest design was to look back at previous identities. Five crests have been used in York City's long history, with varying levels of popularity among supporters. I studied them all, looking to draw inspiration and find reference points. One question we posed in the focus groups, and in the fan survey, was which, of all the club's previous crests, was their favourite? Interestingly, the crest from 1978 to 2002 was overwhelmingly popular with supporters, with over 55 per cent declaring it their preferred design.

'Armed with buckets of inspiration and a newly acquired knowledge of the club's history, I began sketching concepts for the centenary crest. My instinct was to use the fan-favourite design from 1978 to 2002 as the starting point for the sketches. The crest that the club used from 1978 to 2002 featured two stylised lions both facing inwards towards a graphical representation of York's Bootham Bar – an iconic and historic structure in York City centre. I liked this design for its simplicity and symmetry. I also aimed to frame the design in a circular shape. This would represent the completion of a 100-year cycle, and it would reference the famous Pop Stand clock that once stood proudly at Bootham Crescent, the club's beloved old ground. That clock, donated in memory of supporter Phil Dearlove, was recently refurbished and installed in the family zone at the club's brand-new stadium. This sense of old becoming new seemed a fitting element to subtly incorporate into the crest.

'To complete the sketch, I placed typography around the central elements of the design. The top section of the crest clearly displayed the club's name. Then, to avoid cluttering the design, the space at the bottom simply spelt out "100 years". This concept instantly clicked with me. The positioning of the two lions and the city's famous Bootham Bar tower gave the design the balance, strength, and symmetry I was after, while the curvature of the circle seamlessly tied everything together. This rough sketch had outstanding potential, so I transferred it to the computer and began digitising the design.

'So far, I had only seen this design in black and white, so I was keen to add some colour to complete the look. Input from the club's supporters was at the forefront of

my mind throughout the process, but it had a particular influence when deciding on the crest's colours. Fans in the focus groups, and club historian Paul Bowser, had spoken at length about the club's original colours, maroon and white. I realised that maroon would be a great colour to lead with. It spoke of the humble beginnings of the club and would help this crest to stand apart from previous ones. To add a touch of prestige to the design, I added gold. This brought a ceremonial feel to the design and it paired beautifully with the dusky maroon elements. The crest was complete and, to me, it felt perfect for the club and the occasion. But how would the board react?

'After the centenary crest was approved by the club's board, I turned my attention to the design of the club's special edition kit. I had collaborated with Dan Simmonite on the centenary crest project, so it was only natural that we work together on this project too. Dan and I met up to discuss famous York City kits from yesteryear. We covered cult classics and forgotten gems, the legendary moments those kits were involved in, and the various colours the club had worn over the years. It was a fascinating conversation.

'To make this centenary kit extra special, we added a commemorative tag in the lower-right corner of the shirt. This tag adds prestige to the look and feel of the shirt, but it also reinforces that this kit is a special occasion with 100 years of history woven into it. The tag includes a QR code that links the physical product to the digital world. A quick scan instantly transports fans to a web page that documents the football club's journey. I

loved the fact that the kit can represent so much history yet retain the modern touch with QR code technology. Like the centenary crest, it effortlessly connects the old with the new.

'With the kit approved, I worked with sportswear giant Puma to turn my digital design into a physical product of equal quality. Making a success of this kind of transition requires a keen eye for detail. The colours and the placement of the pattern must be exactly right or the whole design will fail. There was a lot of back and forth with Puma as we refined even the smallest details, but it was worth the effort. After all, York City had been waiting 100 years for this kit.

'Working with Dan Simmonite and the York City board of directors was a joy. They gave me an abundance of creative freedom and completely trusted my design decisions. I'm extremely proud of the design that we created. It's unique, stylish, intricate, and relevant to the city of York and its fine football club. I'm confident fans and players alike will embrace a design that is so deeply rooted in their history. I can't wait to see them wearing this once-in-a-lifetime kit as they celebrate a hundred years of York City Football Club.'

The shirts, unsurprisingly, were a smash hit with over 10,000 being sold across the globe and standing testament to an elegant, inclusive and iterative process that fans and staff felt a kinship towards.

14

Icarus: The Value in Having Values

FRONT AND centre of Icarus's website is a mission statement to collaborate on 'a totally unique design that reflects your team's history, values, location and culture'. Their strategy democratises the process of kit creation from a top-down system where you get what you are given to one of collaboration, community and creativity. Their tactics create bold, challenging and often beautifully bonkers designs. Whatever comes of your partnership they tell us how 'it will always be personal'. Rather than only offering a shirt catalogue, their bespoke approach is a blank canvas with the autonomy for clubs and customers to paint their own story, 'We put extensive research into every design, but we also know that no one knows your club better than you. Your dedicated kit design professional will work to incorporate your own ideas within the designs, and you will always have total control over how your club's kit will look.'

They also appreciate how, whether you are a team captain or administrator, the easy part is playing the

game. In Thailand, I used to captain a local side and
the biggest hassle apart from collecting match subs
(and dropping people who would sulk for days; oh, and
booking pitches while navigating Bangkok traffic, and
dodgy referees) was negotiating kit designs with players
who refused to wear certain colours such as those of
rival clubs to those they supported, or had less than

athletic figures (all of us). As a free service, Icarus sets up a shop that crosses one hassle off the list. It helps with collecting each player's contribution (my kit bag loaded with change would mysteriously, consistently, be short of the planned amount and the same suspects would 'need to find an ATM' they never seemed to track down). Icarus also sends the kit out to each player who can log into the shop to order what they need, when they need it. I wish they were around when I needed them, and could run around a football pitch.

Their rallying website cry is 'No More Templates', something they have applied to an astonishing 1,000 global teams since starting out in 2018. In 2020 they relocated to bigger facilities and opened a London office. Building on these strong foundations, July 2023 saw the Icarus Cup take place in founder Robby Smukler's US hometown of Philadelphia to celebrate football's counter-culture of grassroots and independent clubs. Over 80 teams provided more than 1,000 players from

across the US where highly competitive seven-a-side games were counterbalanced by a laid-back festival feel for everything else. Teams were given a free baker's dozen Icarus kits before the tournament, which would not only keep them looking sharp but also make games a canvas for promoting the Icarus designs and tapping into the fan and family networks of all the competing teams. As a man who teaches marketing, I like that idea a lot!

I first came across Icarus in March 2022 when scouting for design companies to create a shirt inspired by a team I used to work for in Thailand. I sourced three possibilities and quickly realised they were the ones for me when Robby got in touch to say how excited they were to bring my Suphanburi FC design to life. People passionate about their business always get my attention and loyalty. I'm a sucker for those who live for what they love. He put me in touch with his designer Jaden

Stevenson, whose energy and sheer joy in playing with the design I have always loved was infectious. He talked me through a range of options that adjusted colour, ratio and all the elements that, in my opinion, make this design one of the most eye-catching and unusual in world football, used by a select number of clubs that includes Canadian Premier League York United FC's 2021 kit and, more famously, Finland's 2020 home shirt (although their cross centres on the Nike swoosh, not the crest). To learn more about this design's story, check out my 'Mighty Fine Design' chapter from *Kit and Caboodle* where the Suphanburi FC president 'Top' talks us through why the shirt means so much to the province he serves. Within a few days, Jaden had given me four choices to consider and, with a few minor adjustments, we came up with a home and away shirt I am proud to wear, share, and for people who have helped me with the book, to give away.

After such a positive experience, I wanted to find out more about what made them tick and, to my delight,

their values aligned with mine. Writing in November 2019, The Athletic's Stephen Wood was also captivated by how Icarus used their designs to create fresh identities for youth and lower-league North American teams. Providence City play in the Bay State Soccer League and focus on promoting local businesses through their values rooted in their community. Their skull and crossbones logo also riffs on the inclusive, creative passion of German club St. Pauli's 'Jolly Roger'. Known as 'Rogues', Providence City proudly play in leagues with the jeopardy of relegation to create a dynamic approach to success and potential failure. Icarus tapped into the values underpinning the club by creating an 'Ocean State Kit' in 2016, a year after the club was formed. I loved how the shirt was designed by one of their players and, after being tested on Twitter (brave souls) it soon picked up traction across the country. I also love the Rogues' outlier attitude that kit design is on par with on-pitch performance. Their partnership with Icarus merged their shared values, rather than sleepwalking towards standard kit design behemoths. (To be fair they are now with Hummel, but the kits are still funky. Their pink with sprinkles design 'Treat Yo Self' kit centred with a massive ad for doughnuts certainly stands out.)

As Robby told Wood, 'It's in a team's best interest to look good. More sponsors, more followers, you sell merchandise. It's a no-brainer.'

Robby has had a lifelong passion for shirts and logos, starting with a childhood researching obscure and random global cities and coming up with fictitious crests for their teams. Later, he started to apply his skills

by producing designs for his friends but, with so much positive feedback, particularly on Instagram, he knew there was a market for his skills and, in 2017, unveiled Icarus FC to the world.

He went on to tell Wood, 'I looked around at the local leagues and saw everyone wearing, you know, Juventus, Munich, popular club jerseys, or the boring Nike or Under Armour or Adidas templates that they give you. I thought my fabric was better than that and I could offer actual customisation that shows off a team's identity.'

2018 was a key year for Icarus when they got their first big order from South Florida United Premier Soccer League side Gold Coast Inter AFC. Robby was doing a 'proper' job at the time to pay the bills but his next order for Philadelphia Lone Star FC in 2020, a team representing expat Liberian players in USL League Two (the fourth tier of American soccer), helped turn a passion project into a business. The bold and distinctly African design not only spoke to the roots of the players' culture but shared a window into the club's personality. It reminded me of the fantastic Grassroot Soccer shirt I mention in this book, which I'm proud to own. He also shared with Wood how the freedom to try new ideas inspired him to follow a less-worn path, including an

Ottoman Empire kit and the designs for a team that played near Chernobyl before the nuclear accident.

I love looking through Robby's imagined historical concept kits for made-up matches between, for example, the Mongol Empire and Conch Republic, as they explain, a tongue-in-cheek Key West micro-nation formed in 1982 by Mayor Wardlow as a protest against the US federal government. As the new prime minister of the Republic, Wardlow declared war against the US (*The Mouse That Roared*-style), surrendered a minute later, and then applied for $1bn in foreign aid. Or how about

Lions of Babylon FC playing away in an extremely funky black kit covered in yellow flowers for, what Icarus tell us is, 'the club's 850th season in the Mesopotamian Premier League' against a feisty Machu Picchu FC on a hot Tuesday evening under (torch) lights. The beauty of these imagined games is that the kits are very real and you can show your support for Umuk Sumerians FC or Hanging Gardens FC by wearing their wonderfully outlandish shirts.

Robby knows that despite the huge resources mega brands like Nike can call on, he occupies a sweet spot where it simply doesn't make financial sense for them to spend their time partnering with clubs to create such detailed work for niche markets when mass-produced, conservative designs will keep their share price cooking. So this frees him and his team up to share their values and flex their design muscles with complete freedom. He told Wood, 'I don't have a million people looking over my shoulder saying you can or can't do this. There's no way I could've done the Chernobyl jersey if I'd had other people looking out.'

One of the many things that appeal to me is that, in a corporate world of safe and high-volume soulless products where margins of safety and rapid planned obsolescence are built into every iteration, people like Robby embrace the chance of potential failure and celebrate the process of taking risks. Even if a design just doesn't make sense, he sees it as worth trying for the sheer fun of it. 2. Bundesliga club Holstein Kiel's third kit for the 2023/24 season had the same motivation, based on construction workers because the club's home

stadium, Holstein-Stadion, was undergoing renovations. The kit paid tribute to the builders helping to enhance the stadium. These are the stories that warm the heart. Robby has ambitions of designing kits for national teams to tap into their rich history and culture. It would need to be a country with an open mind that trusts him with the freedom to play his punk rock football design game but, reviewing his website and my decimated bank account, it would be a sensational sight to behold and a way to re-energise the often staid and risk off approach in national football shirt design.

There was no stopping Icarus in 2023, who partnered with MLS club Philadelphia Union to design a stunning new home kit for the 2023/24 season (I type with one hand and reach for my wallet with the other). The kit was inspired by the city of Philadelphia's history and culture, featuring a blue and gold colour scheme, with a white stripe down the middle of the shirt. They also partnered with Vibes FC, a women's football club based in Austin, Texas, for that season (neighbours to the owners of that stunning purple snakeskin shirt by Sporting Waterloo). The kits were inspired by the city of Austin's music scene. They featured a black and white colour scheme, with a guitar design on the shirt and looked EPIC. True to their values, Icarus launched a new line of custom football kits in late 2023. The kits were available for purchase from the Icarus website, made from recycled materials and were 100 per cent recyclable.

15

ChatGPT – Design Me a Football Kit

IN NOVEMBER 2022, the world seemed unconcerned by the launch of ChatGPT and its (sometimes failing; looking at you, Google) new generation of artificial intelligence competitors/imitators that made Siri look like a confused aunt wrestling with her coins in a long supermarket queue surrounded by tutting teenagers. Not only could it fool your university professor into thinking you wrote that dissertation when you were seen staggering home from this morning's nightclub, but it also claimed to design kits that could pass the football fan's muster. But, a few short months later, Amazon Web Services pumped £100m into the AWS Generative AI Innovation Center which will specialise in integrating AI into an ever-increasing range of daily interactions. In less than a year, we had collectively sleepwalked into a revolution we hadn't even noticed. As Private Frazer would say in *Dad's Army*, 'We're doomed!'

Not much else is more likely to raise the hackles of 'legacy fans' than a computer program touted as knowing what you don't know you want. Relying on technology and being startled by the results is not new. For their 1992/93 shirt, Fiorentina ended up with a series of geometric designs that coalesced to display a swastika.

Fans were even more dismayed because their club had been formed by fascist local politician Luigi Ridolfi after being given an offer you couldn't refuse from Mussolini. The club issued a statement, 'Fiorentina and the manufacturers, Lotto, would like to underline that the optical effect is purely a matter of chance,' blaming a computer program for generating the offensive images. The design was to be binned halfway through the season and replaced with a design less (it could hardly have been more) offensive.

At the cold dead heart of AI football shirt designs sits the omnipresent algorithm that slices our data into bite-sized chunks for businesses feeding off our daily habits and browsing histories. For shirts, it decides how each of the elements will merge. The first step is to hoover up all the data to throw at the process. Here, it could be information taken from training tops, previous kit designs, popular combinations from the past or the palette of colours usually chosen by the club. As long as the images are consistently sized and have similar backgrounds, you can build up your library of potential kit combinations and the algorithm is free to weave its AI magic without being distracted by peripheral non-compliances.

For people looking for the most helpful design data sets, club websites and one of the huge range of passionate football shirt collectors like Gav at Football Kit Geek will give your 'Generative Pre-trained Transformer' all the tools it needs to scrape through data sets in pursuit of logical fits.

Next comes the (fun?) stage of generating the kits. With such a wide range of design images, there is plenty of scope for identifying popular trends and touches. Tethering two algorithms (one for creating the pictures and the other for assessing similarities to the global data set) they become both the pupil and teacher. Algorithm two constantly filters through the work of its partner in a perpetual feedback loop, trying to fool the future wearer into thinking the process was based on old-fashioned concepts like creativity and imagination. The process is intimidatingly data heavy, elbowing aside the insights and allegiances we poor humans cling to. The first result is a visual white noise as the algorithms start warming up for the game ahead. Throwing random pixels at the project like a League Two corner, it then latches on to the shirt's shape before designing doppelgängers of tried and tested combinations and even starts to coalesce around badges and sponsors as it reconstructs the brand born centuries before.

Unfortunately for our data-driven friends, the results tend to fall into three categories that need the human eye and heart to evaluate. Some seem inspired, off-the-wall third shirt potentials, some randomly fall on elegant re-imaginings of a kit's DNA, and a third category careers off into an infinity of dumb ideas and look more like a Sunday league team when the skipper bought the kits online after a particularly long and liquid end-of-season party.

But, for those who see this as, like garlic bread, the future, there are some notes of caution. The vast amount of computing power and time required takes it out of the price and computation range of amateur shirt design explorers with a hunch. Even if you have access to higher computer brainpower, the images will often come out grainy and unfocussed, even after five hours or more using cloud servers' fully flexed computing muscles. Getting past the granular image into the professional-looking could take days of running these systems at full tilt. For us humans feeding the monstrously matrixing machine, there also needs to be a vast data set of shirt images to show a proof of concept. Then comes the additional cost. This vast array of images would need to lean on Amazon Web Services. The daddy of all their offerings, Redshift, comes in at around £5 an hour and, given the time needed, you'd need deep pockets or a consistent income to justify the costs when the results remain tantalisingly uncertain.

The football shirt future isn't what it used to be.

There is something efficiently heartless about this as a way to design kits. After reading about the creative sweat spent on York City, Nairn County and so many other heartfelt designs in this book, the AI process feels like sharing a coffee with Mark Zuckerberg. This experience is also efficient (his dispiriting 'rallying cry' for Meta in 2023) but there is no feeling of human warmth, empathy or inspiration.

A more gentle future-proofing approach was from Brazilian club Atlético Mineiro, which partnered with Le Coq Sportif in 2021 (who I always associate with

Aston Villa's 1981 white glitter shorts). This 'Smart Jersey', called 'Manto da Massa 113' (I love how the 113 'gives a nod' to their centenary. Yes, a nod 13 years in the making) was visually impressive, a design sourced from a fan competition, rather like that of Borussia Dortmund for the 2022/23 season, which celebrates the amazing Westfalenstadion..

The limited-edition shirts also had the added function of an embedded Near-Field Communication tag that lets fans plug themselves into their smartphones (oh joy) and scan the tag for discount coupons and digital content like match highlights for that teeth-gnashing spin-doctoring phrase loved by NFT peddlers, 'fan engagement'. This was something that, in December 2022, third-tier Spanish club Deportivo La Coruña chose to do. Letting them tick the tech and environment boxes, 500 Kappa-designed shirts were made from plastic bottles and various other sea detritus (scientists in March 2023 would report that our poor oceans are choked with 171 trillion pieces of plastic for them to draw from) for their 3-0 victory over Unionistas Salamanca on 8 January 2023. Their NFC also lets wearers source club content and track ownership, which I always thought meant looking in your wardrobe or shouting to your kids about stealing yet another shirt.

The Atlético Mineiro tag was also touted as a way to 'authenticate the purchase', which old-fashioned me thought you did by paying your money for the shirt. It seems strange that in *Kit and Caboodle* I looked back in the 'Wears the Money' chapter on almost exactly this function for Sports Revolution a decade ago in

Thailand but, unfortunately for the company, they had a great idea too early. Like Microsoft's SPOT Watch in 2004, it was doomed to disaster through no fault of its own. The market just wasn't ready. The Mineiro shirt was a huge hit with over 100,000 sold in four days; generating more than three years of match ticket sales is an impressive tally.

The shirt is connected to the club app where 'messages from our sponsors' can be melded into the way fans connect with the club. In a rather saccharine twist, Mineiro prefer to call them 'living jerseys' with built-in planned obsolescence by suggesting that, because every shirt is individually authenticated, one bought in January will be 'different' to one bought a month later. Smells like NFTeen spirit.

16

The Gambler's Remorse

IN MARCH 2023, I spoke to Guy Kilty, AKA Producer Guy, from podcast *The Price of Football*, which had been downloaded an incredible seven million times at the time of typing this. I wanted to learn more about the fantastic design I am honoured to own and the story it tells.

Here's what Guy told me, 'When we were approached by a kit manufacturer who wanted to help us produce a *Price of Football* podcast replica shirt, [co-hosts] Kevin [Day], Kieran [Maguire] and I jumped at the chance. As massive football fans first and foremost, all three of us love strips, both vintage and modern, and we couldn't wait to start designing our own. That process was great fun, but as fans of three different clubs (two of whom hate each other), we had some big decisions to make.

'The first big one was the shirt colour. Kevin supports Crystal Palace, Kieran is a Brighton & Hove Albion fan, and I support Manchester United, so blue and red were both ruled out immediately. We also wanted to make sure we took into account fans who

are colour-blind. Kieran is colour-blind and is often left furious by matches which feature teams whose kits are indistinguishable from one another, so we knew we had to get that aspect right. The obvious choice for them became white. Once we had decided on that, we agreed to add a green and yellow stripe across the middle, in tribute to some of our favourite kits of the past, and add a green and yellow trim to the collar and sleeves. And while we were all happy with that, as always with football fans, you can't please everyone. Shortly after we released the final design, we received messages from Rangers and Ipswich Town fans saying they loved the idea but they'd only be interested in buying an away kit.

'The most fun we had was probably designing the club crest. Spreadsheets and dog snacks were among the many ideas considered for the imagery, but we eventually went for a tasteful illustration of Kieran's dog Finlay and Kevin's cat Smudge. We also created a fake Latin motto, *In Amortise Speramus*, in recognition of our collective love for, and trust in, accountancy, especially amortisation. Finally, we included our fictitious club's name, "Price of Football FC", and the year we started the show, 2019.

'As soon as we'd decided to go ahead with the shirt, we all agreed that the proceeds should go to charity, and there was really only one contender. None of us object to gambling itself – all three of us place bets from time to time – but all of us are concerned about the way the gambling industry advertises its offers constantly during radio and TV broadcasts of football, and fails to adequately look after problem gamblers. That's why we don't run gambling adverts on *The Price of Football*, and it's why we decided to donate all of the profits from the sale of the Price of Football FC replica shirt to Gambling With Lives. It's a community of families bereaved by gambling-related suicide that provides support and raises awareness of gambling's devastating effects and we are all big fans of the work the charity does. Sales of the shirt went really well and we were delighted to be able to hand over the proceeds to a good cause. We were also thrilled to hear about one listener scoring "a hat-trick of worldies" in the shirt in its first outing at five-a-side. Hopefully, we'll get to create another one in the future, maybe a blue and red one for those Ipswich Town and Rangers fans!'

Thanks, Guy. Our friends at The Big Step and Gambling with Lives shared on 29 October 2022 how, in the eight scheduled Premier League games that day, clubs were promoting 30 'official gambling partners'. This is a stunning, depressing fact that Kieran, Kevin and Producer Guy picked up on when designing their Price of Football FC shirts (one of their happy customers happens to be me). The Big Step were delighted that the royalties went to support their incredible work. Guy, Kevin and Kieran were able to hand over £1,240 to help support the fantastic work they do. The charity told me at the end of 2022, 'We're so grateful not just for this very kind gesture, but also for Kieran and Kevin's ongoing support – the advocacy and work they do to raise awareness of gambling harms on the podcast really is invaluable. At Gambling With Lives and The Big Step, we count them as very important supporters! They use their collective voice to speak honestly and comprehensively about the reality that football will not collapse without gambling sponsorship revenue, which is such an important message. We look forward to continuing to work together!'

No bienvenido – Spain's shirt ad ban
Bravely decided during the height of the Covid pandemic, Spanish football chose to stop taking heartbreak money

from gambling companies through shirt sponsorship. Clubs would be allowed to see out existing contracts but that had to be the end of it. This understandably split opinion in an existential time of crisis for the world and threatened to cure the gambling disease but kill the football patient. By March 2022 this meant that, across the top two leagues, a startling 22 clubs were without a main shirt sponsor.

What gives hope to any MPs not sitting in the deep pockets of gambling lobbyists is that, by the start of the 2022/23 season, shirts had been filled with a far healthier range of products and services. However, with the *Masivo Tres* (Spain's big three clubs) safely raking in oceans of shirt sponsorship funds from Emirates, Spotify and Plus500 (although online trading apps often breathe the same air as gambling companies), this seems to drive an even bigger wedge between the haves and the have-yachts. Supply and demand suggest that the other clubs would have had to drop their asking price more readily to potential sponsors with so much shirt space going free across Spanish clubs. But, like any hydra, chopping off one head simply sees another take its place. The reduced profile for shirt front-focussed gambling companies has fostered increasing awareness of gambling addiction's personal and social harms, which has to be applauded. But there has been a net loss in sponsorship revenue and the gambling companies have simply found loopholes to penetrate. Sleeves have less gambling regulation, so some have migrated there. Ad spending has also been diverted into increasing the use of digital sponsorship, where oversight lags behind shirt fronts.

When yet another sordid story surfaced in September 2022 about EFL clubs profiting from the losses of hapless gamblers, it seemed this blight would never leave our game. Documents discovered revealed how clubs had made themselves 'affiliates' so they could take a cut of gamblers' losses with SkyBet. The chances of the Premier League, which had not been opened to scrutiny, doing the same were extremely high. This made the decision by Spanish football to ban shirt advertising of gambling a brave but painful gesture and meant that, for the 2022/23 season, the source of shirt sponsorship had a completely different look. Fifteen per cent of sponsors promoted food and drink (mostly alcohol which clearly also comes with concerns) and four categories each had a ten per cent share of shirts to promote motoring, materials, real estate and telecoms. Worryingly, five per cent of shirts remained sponsorless and Atlético Madrid's sponsorship by cryptocurrency whalefin.com, a company that served notice in February 2023 that it would end its five-year deal as Chelsea's sleeve sponsors less than a year into the deal, only added to the nervousness about partnering with an industry fighting its own existential crisis.

But, depressingly, Spain's stand was very much the exception that proved the rule, although the Netherlands gave us hope in July 2023. The KNVB announced a ban, which is set to take effect in 2025, as part of a wider effort to reduce gambling addiction in the country. It will apply to all levels of Dutch football, from the top professional leagues to the amateur leagues. It will also cover all forms of gambling sponsorship, including shirt sponsorship, stadium naming rights, and advertising on club websites. So there are some embers of hope.

But the next club that careered blindly into the gambling fatberg of sleaze was Aston Villa in early 2023. Despite being dropped as shirt sponsor two years earlier by Norwich City for the sexualised promotion of an already opaque gambling website and having committed to not do precisely what they signed up to do only three months before, BK8 were signed up by Villa on a three-year deal to cheapen their shirt and defile their long and rich history that included supporting the children's end-of-life care charity Acorns. So the number of Premier League clubs sponsored by Asian-facing gambling companies continued to grow as regulators sat on their hands, despite having MP Tracey Crouch's fan-led review ready to address many of the key issues creating such a stain on our shirts.

To appreciate the size of the task facing Crouch's review, we only need to thumb through the gambling hold on club shirts in England's top two divisions. A heartbreaking 40 per cent of Premier League clubs were on the hook to gambling companies. Eight clubs, including the Saudi-owned Newcastle United which contradicts a key tenet of the Muslim religion, chose to swallow their ethics for quick cash. In the Championship, that season saw a quarter of the club shirts promoting gambling, but there were also some enlightened attitudes to the power of our shirt fronts with Wigan Athletic's support of Big Help Project, Burnley promoting the legends at Classic Football Shirts and Bristol City wearing Huboo (more about that later). On promotion to the Championship for 2022/23, Wigan chose not to follow the well-trodden, sordid crypto route where clubs even as big as Manchester City take on the role of the Donald Duck of due diligence (like Manchester City's doomed two-month partnership with crypto firm 3Key Technologies). Instead, at a financial cost but for moral gain, they gave the front-of-shirt spot to Big Help Project, a Liverpool-based charity. Although not seen as a glamorous marketing name, promotion as League One champions and a large fan base in a football heartland would have attracted a reasonable response from cash-rich companies looking to promote their gambling messages by way of a delivery system shirt front. But, despite arriving in what football finance expert Kieran Maguire describes as a 'financial clown car' league where huge wages drive crippling debts, Wigan held firm and chose charity over insanity. Big Help's compelling mission statement in these dark times shows the club made the right decision, 'Our mission is to feed the hungry, overcome poverty, free people from the burden of unmanageable personal debt, help people into affordable housing and to assist people on to a better future.'

Over and above raising awareness for the charity, the club looked to mirror the outreach-focussed approach of their partners. Big Help creates a supportive ecosystem of street-level services for those amid an appalling financial crisis. The shirt sponsorship aimed to triangulate three key stakeholders of the local council, local MPs and

business leaders to drive a raft of community-focussed initiatives that target support for those most at risk. This partnership and approach is a road map for other clubs passively accepting third parties on to their sacred fabric and speaks to a club culture far more meaningful than tax-efficient corporate and social responsibility. Wigan see it, believe it and act on it. More power to their collective elbows, despite a worrying nosedive into League One for 2023/24 trailed by points deductions and concerns for their survival.

Of course, there is the shirt ban on gambling but, rather than an immediate implementation, the rule was kicked into the long grass of the 2026/27 season meaning that the market price was driven even higher by the scarcity of time remaining before gambling companies could pursue the same loopholes explored in Spanish football. Or, as Kieran described it in a tweet shared on 11 July 2023, 'Like a drug addict, Premier League clubs struggle to resist one last payday from the gambling industry.'

Three things made Burnley's 2022/23 shirt sponsorship heartwarming. The first is that Classic Football Shirts are based locally and run by two mates with footy running through their veins. Matthew Dale and Doug Bierton are based in Hyde, Manchester, and have been running their business for 16 years. The second, delicious reason for celebration is who they replaced on the shirt. Online casino, turbo bankrupting contracts for differences and fixed odds betting pushers Spreadex certainly didn't speak to the club's values or that of their highly intelligent and universally respected manager Vincent Kompany. Sadly, the third reason this season was so special was that it bookended W88, the 'leading sports betting and online casino operator' who would come back to haunt the shirt for 2023/24.

It, fleetingly, restored faith in humanity when, rather than flashy betting-disguised-as-investment moving northwards in exponential and socially harmful ways, it was a company like Classic Football Shirts seeing turnover jump from £11.9m to £18.2m during that 2022/23 financial year and its pre-tax profits went from £1.3m to £3.8m. Burnley chairman Alan Pace, rather than the usual rictus smile of a custodian accepting heartbreak money, warmly welcomed a visitor to the club shirt that everyone can be proud of, 'We all appreciate how important kits are to fans. Classic Football Shirts epitomise this. A football kit can ignite memories and take you back to a special moment in an instant, this is why we are delighted to make a nod to our history with this year's retro-style home kit and partnering with Classic Football Shirts is the perfect fit.'

Bristol City's partnership with Huboo is one more reason to be proud of living in the West Country. This local (which always gets me onside) fulfilment company not only took the shirt spot for the Robins for an initial three years but four other professional sports teams in the local area for the 2022/23 season and beyond. This group is made up of the City men and women, rugby club Bristol Bears' men and women as well as the Bristol Flyers basketballers. It was almost quaint in our world of offshored, ghostship, white label sponsorships by unregulated shell companies to hear Huboo's co-founder share with the official club media, 'We're proud to call Bristol home and are honoured to partner with such a prestigious sporting group which is so fundamental to this city.'

Now facing the multi-club multiverse of the City Group and their imitators looking to strangle competition at birth around the globe, this type of protective umbrella across different sports in the same city is a welcome outlier. Formed in 2014, Bristol Sport sees the football, rugby and basketball clubs as different cogs driving the same machine, not for global domination but for local pride and well-being driven through shared values and aspirations. As with Burnley's brief dalliance with sanity, this new partnership even has the added authenticity of kicking a four-year gambling shirt sponsorship into the long grass. Dunder Casino (based in both Malta and Curaçao for double the protection from oversight and taxation) in 2018 was followed by MansionBet coming to you out of Gibraltar.

Hope is the last thing to die. A small, committed and increasingly vocal chorus of voices in the game was starting to build traction through a simple, but profoundly clear message. If gambling companies throw oceans of money at the game to buy legitimacy, then let's get paid less and enjoy the game more. Former Exeter City favourite David Wheeler wrote in a January 2023 edition of *The Guardian* a powerfully framed manifesto. No ifs, no buts: kick gambling out of the game. The ready, fire, aim strategy of gambling behemoths flooding the game has created an alternative reality where shirts are assumed to be easy prey to their gateway drug of football, leading to the terminal velocity of slots and casino-based games that rinse initiated and dumb money alike.

As David reviewed his decade-long career and 500 professional appearances (149 of them for Exeter) he reflected on how, for almost every one of those appearances, he has worn or been surrounded by online casino adverts. In his typically eloquent way, David expanded on the consequence of this gambling saturation, 'Behind this bombardment of marketing, most of us know someone who has struggled with gambling because this addiction can happen to anyone. The harms can devastate every part of someone's life, and those closest to them, with huge long-term cost to society.'

David stands fully behind Tracey Crouch's fan-led review as a reset for the game that was started by clubs like David's first, Lewes FC, which I reviewed in *Kit and Caboodle*, and the baton picked up by our friends at Gambling With Lives who inspired Kevin Day and Kieran Maguire to share all profits from their Price of Football FC shirts with them.

Even broadcasters are now starting to question why every shirt sponsor is given a free pass, whatever it is trying to sell. In early January 2023, BeiN Sport cancelled the transmission of Atalanta's game against Bergamo due to 'prohibited advertising' on Atalanta's shirts. Plus500 has promoted risky financial instruments through its opaque headquarters of Cyprus with impunity across global shirts including Atlético Madrid and Legia

Warsaw. This shot across the bows by the authorities might just give it pause to think that sometimes, if rarely, some will hold them to a higher standard than 'where's my cash?'. In this gambling-controlled universe, it was also comforting to read about the innovative Greek amateur team Voukefala. Faced with losing the €12,000 they needed each season to keep afloat they turned to one of the few businesses thriving in the region: Madam Soula's brothels. Righteous indignation poured down from many for a club based in a league sponsored by the state-owned lottery and betting company OPAP. The team's president, Ioannis Batziolas pithily struck to the heart of the league's hypocrisy, 'What is the better idea to promote? Gambling or sex?'

17

Love is Love

ON VALENTINE'S Day in 2023, my Exeter
City showed their commitment to the Football v
Homophobia campaign when the visit of Shrewsbury
Town to St James Park was dedicated, for the 14th
time (appropriately) as the annual fixture focussing
on a communal stand against homophobic attitudes.
Driven by Proud Grecians, whose banner is a permanent
fixture on the stadium perimeter, and Exeter Pride, the
game was a showcase and rallying cry for the values
our trust-owned club holds dear. Players warmed up
in Football v Homophobia T-shirts, and flyers, stickers
and welcoming friendship was offered throughout the
evening. Our media officer and programme editor Craig
Bratt is a stalwart of support for all LGBTQ+ groups and
shows an open, respectful and professional attitude that
makes my club so special.

Proud Owls

The beauty of stunningly designed kits is how they grab
your attention and make you want to find out more

about the people behind them (and in them). At work, I teach my students a concept called AIDA – Attention, Interest, Desire, Action. Scrolling through the torrents of information/disinformation on Twitter, standout shirt designs make us pause and briefly capture our attention. Seeing the Proud Owls' messages on the front and back of their shirt, the level of detail and the story behind each design decision piqued my interest to find out more about their values. Then, after contacting them and feeling the huge passion they have for the LGBTQ+ community and the love they all share of Union Omaha, they fuelled a desire to learn more about what drives, binds and inspires them. Unfortunately, I missed out on the presale deadline to take action and own one of these beauties, but it is only a matter of time.

I spoke to the group in March 2023 and asked them to tell me more about their group. Here is what they shared with me, 'Proud Owls is an independent supporters' group for Omaha, Nebraska's professional, USL League One club, Union Omaha. Proud Owls was started with the intent of supporting Union Omaha, while also providing representation for LGBTQIA+ Union Omaha fans and allies. Among the values adopted by Union Omaha is the idea that "One Means All" and that soccer is a game for everyone. Proud Owls believes it is its responsibility to hold the club responsible for upholding its motto that "One Means All", particularly as it relates to issues important to the LGBTQIA+ community.

'Proud Owls began on 1 June 2022, but has quickly established itself with the club itself and within the supporter community. Proud Owls regularly partners with the other Union Omaha supporters' groups and has been accepted as a key member of the supporter culture in Omaha. Proud Owls is an affinity supporters' group, meaning it is open to anyone concerned with LGBTQIA+ issues, especially in soccer and soccer supporter culture, whether members of any other Union Omaha supporters' groups and irrespective of personal identity or orientation. Proud Owls welcome allies, as well as those who identify as LGBTQIA+. It is Proud Owls' goal to make the entire Union Omaha experience

as welcoming and inclusive as it can be and to ensure the club lives up to that goal as well. It is Proud Owls' goal to grow its group within the Union Omaha community and to use its members' passion to better the Omaha community, the soccer community and to assist the LGBTQIA+ community.

'With respect to its kit, Proud Owls had the good fortune of working with Olive & York and specifically Zephyros Designs. It was inspired by a corn kit the club jokingly suggested it would make. Because some of the supporters from rival clubs joke about Omaha and its relationship with corn, Proud Owls decided to walk into the joke and use the idea of heirloom rainbow corn as the central design element of the kit. Adding the club's traditional colours, "lightning" and black, to the rainbow corn combined pride in multiple ways, pride in the club, as well as LGBTQIA+ pride reflected by the rainbow corn. The final design element was to make a human rights statement that is particularly important in these times, specifically the need to "Protect Trans Lives". Thus, the kit was intended to show support for Union Omaha, pride in the LGBTQIA+ community, and to advocate for an important cause, the need to protect transgender lives.

'Finally, in an effort to support a local chapter of an organisation committed to protecting and advocating for the LGBTQIA+ community, particularly queer youth, Proud Owls offered the traditional "sponsor" spot on its kit to the Omaha chapter of GLSEN. GLSEN is a national organisation that works to "ensure that every member of every school community is valued and respected regardless of sexual orientation, gender identity or gender expression". Because Proud Owls is committed to issues of queer representation, and that representation is particularly essential with respect to queer youth, Proud Owls found the partnership with GLSEN Omaha to fit perfectly with its mission. In addition to the shirt sponsor spot, all net proceeds from the sale of Proud Owl kits were donated to GLSEN Omaha to support its mission.'

The shirt got through to the last 16 of Olive & York's Kit of The Year competition but had the bad luck to be drawn against the Ukrainian national team. Even then, they managed to collect 40 per cent of the 900 votes after soundly beating the Massachusetts Tabby

Cats FC by 26 per cent to reach the last 16. Rarely has a shirt combined a standalone beauty, told an inspiring story and brought together a group of open-minded, supportive and enabling people like this. Proud Owls may be small, but their cause is mighty.

Football v Homophobia – promoting inclusivity in the beautiful game

Launched in 2010, Football v Homophobia aims to create a safe and welcoming environment for LGBTQ+ individuals, including players, fans, and staff. One of its key contributions is the design and promotion of the FvH shirt, which serves as a powerful symbol of solidarity and support for the LGBTQ+ community in football. The design often incorporates vibrant colours, including the iconic rainbow flag, the symbol of LGBTQ+ pride. The campaign recognises the power of football as a unifying force and leverages its influence to challenge discrimination and promote understanding.

The FvH shirt goes beyond being a mere article of clothing. It plays a crucial role in raising awareness about the importance of inclusion and respect within the football community. By wearing the shirt, people send a clear message that homophobia has no place in football. The shirt's visibility on the pitch and in stadiums helps amplify the campaign's message, reaching a broad audience and sparking conversations about LGBTQ+ inclusion.

Clubs and players who wear the shirt demonstrate their commitment to promoting inclusivity, equality, and diversity in football. This visible show of support encourages LGBTQ+ individuals to feel welcomed and accepted within the football community. It sends a powerful message that everyone, regardless of their sexual orientation or gender identity, has a place in the beautiful game. Beyond its symbolic value, the shirt serves as a means to generate funds for the campaign's ongoing work. Proceeds often contribute to supporting educational initiatives, awareness programmes, and resources that combat homophobia and discrimination in football. Football v Homophobia, through its various initiatives, has played a pivotal role in raising awareness and combating discrimination. The campaign fosters dialogue, educates the football community, and promotes acceptance. By challenging prejudiced beliefs and emphasising inclusivity, Football v Homophobia ensures that everyone can enjoy the beautiful game without fear of discrimination or prejudice based on their sexual orientation or gender identity.

Stonewall FC – empowering LGBTQ+ inclusion through a symbolic shirt

Stonewall FC is a prominent LGBTQ+ football club based in London. Founded in 1991, it holds the distinction of being the world's most successful gay football club. Stonewall FC not only provides a platform for LGBTQ+ people to participate in football but actively advocates for LGBTQ+ inclusion in the sport. As part of their efforts to promote their cause and raise awareness, Stonewall FC designed a unique shirt that has become an iconic symbol of their club and their commitment to LGBTQ+ rights. The shirt features a bold design that incorporates the rainbow flag with its vibrant colours prominently displayed. These colours represent the inclusivity and acceptance of all sexual orientations and gender identities.

The Stonewall FC logo is often featured on the shirt, along with any relevant sponsorship or branding. The shirt serves multiple purposes for Stonewall FC. Firstly, it is worn by the players during matches, representing their team and their dedication to the sport. By proudly displaying the rainbow flag on their shirts, the players demonstrate their commitment to LGBTQ+ visibility and equality in football. Secondly, the shirt acts as a symbol of support for the LGBTQ+ community, both within and beyond the football world. It serves as a visual representation of Stonewall FC's mission to challenge homophobia and discrimination in sport. By wearing the shirt, the players and the club aim to inspire others and encourage a more inclusive and accepting environment in football.

The design has attracted attention and recognition both within and outside the LGBTQ+ community. It has become an emblem of Stonewall FC's activism and a symbol of progress in the ongoing fight against homophobia and prejudice in sports. The shirt sparks conversations, challenges stereotypes, and inspires other clubs and organisations to take a stand against homophobia and discrimination. Stonewall FC's shirt has also played a role in fundraising efforts. The club often sells replica shirts to supporters, with proceeds going towards funding their activities and initiatives. This allows fans and supporters to show their solidarity with Stonewall FC and contribute to the club's ongoing work in promoting LGBTQ+ inclusivity.

18

Mind Always Matters

A HEARTBREAKING and deeply powerful YouTube video came out at the end of 2019 from Mind, the mental health charity. In it, stories of deep sadness and massive courage were shared and shirts became the catalyst for, at times, simply being able to put one foot in front of the other. The narrator Sean Jarvis (who was the commercial director of Huddersfield Town at the time) shared the heartbreaking story of his nephew's suicide, reflecting on the statistic of how one in four people are battling some form of mental health issue. The story was then taken up by former Burton Albion midfielder Ben Fox, whose career-ending injury caused him mountains of mental anguish. He revealed his reaction to being given the devastating news by the team physio, 'I just burst into tears, just didn't know what to do, just didn't have it.'

For Huddersfield's first team coach Mark Hudson, the suicide of his wife's sister showed him the importance of talking, sharing and community. He admitted, 'I felt very uncomfortable in social surroundings but the

longer I've talked about it the more I feel OK talking about it, the better I feel every time I talk about it and the more I started to open up.'

The video's key message is to notice the squiggle on the back of EFL shirts, have your mate's back and turn your shirt around to show you care so the Mind logo is facing the world instead of being hidden over your shoulder. To focus attention on this terrible burden often carried by those least able to cope, there is a Mental Health Awareness Week each May. In 2022, the National Football Museum in Manchester hosted an exhibition celebrating four years of the 'On Your Side' campaign between Mind and the EFL. It was a chance to celebrate the 7,000 matches where club shirts bore the Mind logo and the 93 dedicated Mind matches. The overseers of league football often come in for justified criticism of their stewardship but this initiative deserves universal praise, illustrated by the example of Cameron Miller, who first reached out for help from Mind. When he saw their squiggle on the back of Charlton Athletic's kit he 'felt like I'd been given permission to start on my journey to getting support'.

Mental Health Football

Mental Health Football is a group based in Oldham whose mission statement is 'to improve attendees' mental health using football and peer support'. I was honoured to contact Ross Elliott and hear his story and that of his MHF support that typifies the struggles and solutions that the group seek to address and share.

Ross said, 'I've been involved in football my whole life, playing at home, at school and with my mates. When I wasn't playing football, I was playing *Championship Manager* or watching Manchester City. When I was 15, I joined my first open-age team; what I didn't know at that time was that my mum was ill with early onset Alzheimer's. By the age of 21 I had quit work to look after her. Football at the weekends and midweek piss-ups with my mates (once my dad had returned home from his job) got me through.

'When I was 23, my mum died, aged 53. Three days after her death I played for my team at the weekend. I didn't mention it to any of my team-mates, I just wanted the escape that football can bring. As time went by, I relied less on the piss-ups and more on the football, playing or training four or five times a week. Our

shared love of Manchester City had also given me, my dad, and my brother a connection that helped us through the grieving process. Without football, it felt like we'd have had little to talk about. I have always believed in football being a force for good and over the years as I took on more responsibility at AFC Oldham (player, captain, first team manager and committee member). I wanted to use that power to help others feel part of something.'

In 2018, based on their personal experiences and experiences in amateur football, Ross Elliott and his fellow AFC Oldham joint first team manager Andy Steel began conversations about holding a free weekly game of football in a pressure- and judgement-free environment.

The game would use physical activity and peer support to allow attendees to play, or watch and have a chat, and improve their mental health.

Mental Health Football began in January 2019, and the premise was clear: no expectations, no scorelines, no winners or losers, no sign-up or commitment necessary. Seven attended the first session and it's grown from there. Such was Andy's belief in MHF that he funded most of the early sessions with extra financial support coming from Ross, as well as the odd attendee and friends and family.

In October 2019, MHF went on to win the Initiative of the Year award at the Oldham Sports Awards, followed by the runners-up spot at the North West Sports Awards. In 2020, Ross designed a new MHF badge using the AFC Oldham colours – orange, black and white. It contains the silhouette of a head on a white background with the letters 'MHF' and the white of the football bringing light out of the darkness. The new badge coincided with a move to a bigger venue to accommodate the increasing number of attendees.

2021 was a massive year for MHF, and in May that year the group was invited to its first tournament, a big deal for an initiative that is based on non-competitive sessions. The tournament was aimed at raising awareness of mental health, and MHF were delighted to be involved, playing against similar initiatives and a celebrity team featuring former Bolton and Celtic player Alan Thompson and Steve Rotheram, the Metro Mayor of the Liverpool City Region. They got knocked out in the group stages but made a lot of new friends.

AFC Oldham supported by loaning MHF their Hope and Glory-manufactured home kit for the day. Ross and Andy wanted it to be clear that this was an MHF team, not an AFC Oldham one, and so Ross quickly designed an MHF flag. The white flag with its MHF badge sitting on an orange and black sash immediately became an important part of MHF, a symbol that helped attendees feel part of something. To this day, they proudly pose with the flag at the end of each weekly session (in June 2022, Ross and Andy launched MHW, a mental health walking initiative for those who prefer a walk and talk), and in August, and with attendances at sessions regularly between 20 and 30, Manchester FA announced MHF as their Grassroots Project of the Year. New funding soon followed which would allow MHF to evolve further.

In 2022, MHF moved to a bigger venue, again. New branded bibs arrived in May. In July, MHF entered another mental health awareness tournament, new allies were made and in September a friendly was organised at Gigg Lane against like-minded club Place 2 Place FC. It was an amazing day and part of an incredible journey for MHF attendees who got to play in a famous stadium in front of family and friends. AFC Oldham supported both events with an away kit loan.

In December, due to an increased awareness of the project, and the many offers of friendlies flooding in, discussions began about MHF having their very own kit. Andy, Ross, MHF volunteers and attendees all agreed that an MHF team was a great idea, but that it would take part in friendly fixtures only, with raising

awareness of mental health the priority. The team would never be about winning at all costs or putting out the best players, but about being inclusive and open to all MHF attendees (a current age range of 18 to 72). Plans were also announced to launch a women's MHF session starting in 2023.

Ideas for the MHF kit were floated around between attendees and volunteers, and Hope and Glory who would produce it. Early visuals had an AFC Oldham feel with orange being the most prominent colour, but Ross and Andy wanted the kit to be simple and clean, in MHF colours and with a design relatable to attendees. The answer was obvious: use the one design that symbolises that the attendees are in it together, that they are united in the cause.

And so MHF approached Hope and Glory about a sash kit to match their iconic flag. An obvious thing to do at this stage would have been to attract a front of shirt sponsor and raise some money towards the kit, but this was never considered. The focus would be on Mental Health Football only. After an open chat with our attendees, it was decided though that MHF would carry a logo and phone number on the rear of the shirts. Samaritans have our back.

The MHF kit was launched in January 2023 on the fourth anniversary of MHF with a mental health awareness friendly against a like-minded initiative, Happy Somedays FC. In the four years it has been running MHF has won awards, started a walking group, launched a new kit, begun a women's session and worked together with other mental health groups and initiatives. But most importantly, MHF has created friendships and helped those with depression, anxiety, and social isolation, among other problems and issues.'

Their shirts started to focus minds on being well in the 2021/22 season. The limited-edition shirt retailed at £29.99 and a third of its proceeds helped the charity use football as therapy for those battling the 'black dog' of depression. By buying and wearing this incredibly stylish sash shirt, we (and I count myself as one of its

happy customers) are also making a stand against the semi-skimmed creations we are expected to buy that are full of commercial sound and fury, but signify nothing. As importantly, they encourage engagement and conversations and help fund tournaments that develop further support networks. Boxer Tyson Fury has long been an open advocate of sharing mental health challenges after his precipitous fall into being unwell, and his sponsorship of local club Morecambe's shorts shows another way our kits can talk to us about subjects that we all draw on at times in our lives.

2023 saw MHF power ahead with a vast range of projects, driven by the huge boost of being nominated for the 2023 Charity of the Year honour given by the Oldham Business Awards. The same year also saw them launch a new campaign to raise awareness of mental health in football. The campaign, called Heads Up, encouraged people to talk about their mental health and to seek help if they need it. The campaign was supported by several professional footballers, including former Manchester United and England defender Gary Neville. They also partnered with the Oldham Athletic Community Trust to deliver a new mental health programme for young people. The Mindful Kickabout uses football to teach young people about mental health and how to cope with stress and anxiety. It is funded by the National Lottery Community Fund. It is wonderful to see this group going from strength to strength, providing the care and compassion so often lacking in our Tory-infested world.

Mental Health Week is marked in May each year and was supported by a man not known for making good news off the field. Manchester City and England defender Kyle Walker collaborated with suicide prevention charity CALM (Campaign Against Living Miserably) to design limited-edition home and away kits that were showcased in the *FIFA '22* video game and available to buy from fellow collaborators Puma and Pro:Direct Soccer. The design walks us through Walker's career (the parts that can be shown on a family shirt) with a palette from each of the clubs he has played for as a tribute to making him the person and father he has become. The away shirt takes a more jagged view of the problems facing those of us dealing with poor mental health, using statistics and phrases conveying how over 100 people take their own lives in the UK every week, with three-quarters of them being male. The kit also carries CALM's mantra, 'Life is always worth living.' Walker shared an eloquent and heartfelt reason for joining the project when describing how to 'create these kits is a reminder that no matter what you're going through, there's always hope and always someone to lean on'.

Also speaking to club and manufacturer values is a commitment by our friends at Loch Ness FC to supporting Mikeysline, a grassroots mental health and suicide prevention charity, through a percentage of revenue generated from their kit sales. They were able to hand over £537 during a mental health awareness week in 2023.

Mikeysline was set up in 2015 after two friends, Martin Shaw and Michael Williamson, died in two devastating days, highlighting the growing trend of Highlands suicides. At that time, for those dealing with depression, there was nowhere to go for advice and support. So founder Ron Williamson, Michael's uncle, decided to act. There was immediate support and gratitude for the fifth emergency service that listens without judgement. Their overarching approach is to break down the stigma about asking for help with our mental health and how it is OK not to be OK. In a shirt world daubed with foetid crypto carpetbaggers, we should all pause, applaud, and support this partnership between football shirts and mental wellness. West Ham fans who fell for their club's officially sanctioned 'Decentralised Asset Management Partner' Peak (oh, the irony) must be green with envy. Those who, as reported by the legend that is Martin Calladine invested £100 at its launch in May 2022 would be sitting on a nest egg of £2.30 a year later. Madness.

Loch Ness wasn't the only club to support this incredible cause of Mikeysline. Nairn County not only wear kits for TeamHamish as I shared earlier, but their home shirt for the 2022/23 season had the Mikeysline logo on the back, part of a two-season partnership started in June 2022. Each November there is also a memorial match between Loch Ness and Inverness Athletic to celebrate the life of Donald (D.J.) Macphee, who played for both clubs before his untimely death. The match also raises money for Mikeysline. On 2022's World Mental Health Day, on 17 October, Ross County also used their warm-up shirts to promote the Mikeysline legends, as would Scottish Championship side Inverness Caledonian Thistle for their warm-up before facing Queen's Park in March 2022.

These are the values shared further south in England's Midlands, where Mind, Body & Sole's director and founder Adam G. told me about the power of their shirts to spread awareness of mental health issues after setting the group up in January 2021, 'MBS have partnered up with kit supplier Fused Sport for this football shirt that we designed to raise awareness for mental health. One hundred per cent of the profits are being donated to a Stoke-based food bank called Affordable Food. Mind, Body & Sole is a non-profit organisation based in Congleton that currently works with three non-league clubs raising awareness for

mental health in the communities with three drop-in centres too. We offer financial and emotional support worldwide and raise funds by selling our products which range from T-shirts, hoodies, sweatshirts and long sleeves. It really is an honour to have such a beautifully made football shirt catching people's eyes who wouldn't normally look out for MBS.'

The shirt was a real stunner (I should know; I bought one) and helped reach new groups with its supportive, inclusive and collegial approach not only to supporting those dealing with mental health issues but, through their football merchandise, to raise funds that are shared with people who are dealing with financial burdens that further affect their mental health.

19

Hatch, (Football) Match
and Dispatch

Hatch

In chapter four of *Kit and Caboodle* (thanks so much to all of you who bought it) I looked back on the enlightened and community-building marketing strategy of the Italian club Atalanta. Aware of not drawing from the heft and history of their close neighbours in Milan, they identified a unique selling point of their region: pride. To amplify this sense of place and identity, they issued all newborn children in the area and beyond shirts showing their allegiance to The Goddess. Fast forward to 2023 and the club renowned for fighting way above their financial weight class seems to have started something.

For San Marino, FIFA ranking rock bottom-dwellers looking up in envy to Anguilla and the British Virgin Islands, even their official Twitter account describes them with a whiff of patronising fatalism as 'the bravest football team in the world'. By July 2023 they had failed to win in their last 130 games. With a population the size of Windsor to call on who live in a territory covering only 40 square miles (making it only slightly larger than Lincoln), their only option is to build from within. So, from December 2022 to the end of 2023 every newborn baby was to be draped in the micro-nation's shirt as a way of inspiring a new nappied legion (with a population growth of around 250 in 2022 it is more of a squad). This is a heartfelt but small gesture as this country based in, and dominated by, Italy. The national team has also been dominated by pretty much everyone they have played since first playing in 1986 with, by the summer of 2023, a record of 186 losses and nine draws including a 1-1 stalemate with St Lucia at the end of November 2022, making it an undefeated three days before losing to the same opponents after 72 hours of basking in the glory. But they have won a game, trivia buffs – a 1-0 friendly victory over Liechtenstein on 18 April 2004. When your all-time top scorer has eight and his closest challenger has two, you have to look elsewhere for a feeling of achievement through gallows humour. 'The Never One Joy Brigade' can boast up to a dozen members at matches drawn to the bleak thrill of watching success being measured in corners or long-range shanks, but also in unique experiences. After a goalless draw at home to Estonia in a Euro 2016 qualifier in November 2014 (the first time in a decade they had dodged defeat) the players invited the group to a party at a nearby bar. Surely the heady reflections on a goalless draw have rarely been enjoyed with such gusto.

Nearer to home, League of Ireland Premier Division club Sligo Rovers decided in March 2021 to harness pamper power too, with all locally born babies given free team jerseys as they closed in on a century of survival thanks to fierce local pride being passed down generations through their trust status that gives fans complete control of the club and (like my trust-owned Exeter City) converts a crowd to a community. Like other clubs seeking enlightened ownership over nation state sports back channelling, success is survival occasionally sprinkled with on-pitch success. In their 95 years, Sligo have won three league titles, five FAI Cups and two League Cups. A ground for 5,000 people creates a close-knit sense of knowing your fans and neighbours on a chilly Saturday (or even chillier Tuesday night). So, every new baby born at Sligo University Hospital was part of a campaign that gave away 1,000 shirts. Driven by the passion and commitment of their supporters' trust, the Return on Vestments will take years to arrive, but the club faced an existential pandemic crisis that was only averted thanks to a community contribution of €400,000. Unlike so many modern club shirts blighted by gambling and their shadow-fellow cryptos, the shirts also promoted an Irish mortgage provider, Avant Money, who stepped in as part of the rescue package. Although too young to notice, the babies are making a small but heartfelt statement that shirts still have the potential to share a message of hope over cynicism.

Rovers CEO Colin Feehily shared how the club was 'very happy to be bringing extra smiles to those in Sligo University Hospital'. He also expressed gratitude to the hospital's employees for their work during the Covid-19 pandemic. The jersey giveaway was a great success, and it was so popular that it continued through 2022. In that year, even more jerseys were produced free of charge for families during their stay at Sligo University Hospital. Sligo Rovers' jersey giveaway was a heartwarming gesture that showed the club's commitment to its community. It was a great way to welcome new babies into the world and introduce them to the club's rich history and tradition.

(Football) Match

Nick Hornby's 1997 film *Fever Pitch* pinpointed the dilemma for many football fans. Matches have a rhythm and regularity, nailed down by the fixture list, but life is frustratingly fluid. Colin Firth's Paul Ashworth and Ruth Gemmell's Sarah Hughes are now considered to be in a stable, long-term relationship but, compared to Paul's love of Arsenal, they have merely added pressure to an already overcrowded fixture list. This exchange beautifully illustrates the football fan's potential separation anxiety each time a non-football-focussed fixture is introduced into their lives. Births, marriages and deaths are more unnecessary complications to seasons that must be followed in full.

Sarah:

We've been … seeing each other – well, we've been sleeping together for six months now. And we've never even planned a holiday together. It's a miracle if we plan a weekend before Friday afternoon. And yet you know what Arsenal are doing for months in advance.

Paul:

They produce a fixture list.

Sarah:

Well, I can do that for you. Give me your diary and I'll put some dates in it.

Paul:

Don't be daft.

Sarah:

What's daft about it?

Paul:

I don't really see the difference.

Sarah:

How about Saturday, October the eighth? Let's go away somewhere.

Paul:

I haven't got next season's fixture list yet.

Sarah:

You know you're seeing Arsenal next year. You can't say whether you'll be seeing me.

Paul:

So what? Everyone's like that. You know you'll be seeing your sister next season.

Sarah:
Sisters don't have seasons.

Paul:
Whatever.

At the end of December 2022 Sachin R. and R. Athira in the southern Indian state of Kerala made football central to their ceremony. Both of them appeared in World Cup shirts. The happy groom wore the shirt of champions Argentina, but for his bride, it was the colours of the frustrated finalists, France. Wisely, they got the boring stuff out of the way first, completing the ceremony before kick-off (for those of us who have been to Indian weddings, it feels like the end of the ceremony and the first anniversary could merge). Unsurprisingly, both went for the iconic names and number tens of M and M: Messi and Mbappe.

For such a (normally) happy day it's fitting that football can offer a chance to share a different kind of passion between newlyweds. I invited Paul McGrath to my wedding but, luckily for my wife (I did call out 'I love you' when his card apologising for his no-show was read out) he couldn't make it. When football makes up so much of our life's journey, it simply seems fitting that every stop along its way should be celebrated by renewing our vows that, next season for sure, we will go up.

Appropriately published on Valentine's Day 2023, The Athletic, the authoritative website for football journalism, took a peak at what it was like getting married at a football stadium on a Saturday, with a 3pm kick-off (already making their marriage rarer than most club fixtures in modern football). Reporters Nick Miller and Nancy Frostick described a ceremony that, to the horror of grumpy groundsmen everywhere, was completed in the centre circle of Wembley Stadium. Adrian and Wendy Steel decided to get married in 2003, but it wasn't until four years later that the 'home of English football' had been rebuilt so, rather than try for the Mansfield Town-loving groom's Field Mill, they waited. And waited. With all the Wembley delays, they would go on to have two children before their constantly rearranged fixture. When the day finally arrived, everyone came in kits of their own clubs. Wendy and the bridesmaids wore England-themed wedding clothes and Adrian wore an England kit, with the three lions crest replaced by the Mansfield stag and, of course, the day and date of this encounter embroidered into his shirt.

Dispatch

Christopher Walken as Frank Featherbed, an American interloper in the sleepy Welsh village of Wrottin-Powys, was determined to revolutionise the undertaking business in Britain through the innovation of 'themed funerals' in the darkly brilliant 2006 comedy *Undertaking Betty*. 'The root word of funerals is fun … funeral fashion. It's the next big thing.' As I did for my dad, draping his coffin in his favourite club shirt is a way to make our final connection, but there is so much more that an often bleak ceremony can offer to show how the beautiful game can send us off in style.

It's our chance, for a final time, to celebrate a lifelong love. From the football shirt wreaths to a casket with our club crest on, the four horsemen can pause a moment while we reflect on a player down. Some clubs even take over the whole ceremony for you. Edinburgh's Heart of Midlothian invite us to book their Tynecastle Park stadium for funerals and 'celebration of life events'. Using up to six VIP suites, their club staff are on hand to provide support. They even have a tastefully designed brochure (should it be a 'dispatch day programme'?) that talks potential customers through their unplanned and unwanted potential purchases. No mention is made of where ashes can be scattered after the ceremony (should we have splurged on the Scottish steak pie with puff pastry instead of playing safe with option four's selection of mini pies?).

But at some funerals, it isn't only the living who choose to focus on their footy. In February 2023 lifelong referee Bob Fielding sadly died at 89. The Peterborough local's 'life was football' according to his grieving family. So much so that, when he married his late wife Sheila, he made her wait on the touchline in her wedding dress before they set off for their honeymoon. After four decades working the whistle, his last decision was to be cremated in his referee kit. The family also encouraged mourners to wear their favourite football kits at the ceremony.

20

Corinthians: Wearing Their Hearts on Their Sleeves

AS WE watch 22 global corporations circle each other on a Premier League matchday, there is something refreshingly prelapsarian about clubs pursuing a higher, communal purpose. Now playing in the Isthmian League South Central Division after their recent relegation from the Premier League, Corinthian Casuals are 'dedicated to amateurism' and through a sense of community that a level financial playing field (i.e., most clubs are skint) promotes. Although written a century ago, this description of the club by R. Robinson in his book *History of the Queen's Park Football Club* still resonates with those of us looking to support football teams rather than nation states seeking petrochemical soft power:

'The Corinthians, a band of amateurs – and such amateurs! A brilliant galaxy of talent ... whose sole aim and ambition were to bring out all that is good and healthy in a pastime they followed for the love of it ... the name of the club is, even at the present day, a household word for all that is chivalrous, clean, upright and true in the civilised world of sport.'

But there was more to the Corinthians than this determination to uphold an amateur ethos. As David Goldblatt describes it in his definitive book on football's history, *The Ball is Round*:

'The Corinthians played a self-consciously buccaneering, free-spirited attacking football that was emblematic of an older golden era of aristocratic sporting, political and ideological dominance.'

Spanning the globe with these shared values, after the English club visited Sao Paulo in 1910 Brazilian locals were inspired to establish a club that has become a global giant playing in a 50,000-capacity stadium and an average attendance of 43,481, the highest in Serie A in the 2023/24 season and 43,293 higher than their Mother Club. Sport Club Corinthians Paulista may be a financial behemoth, with *Forbes* valuing their team at £317 million in May 2020 and an operating income of £8.8 million but its conduct is predicated on those shared values of its Mother Club playing Thatcham Town and Binfield on desolate January afternoons. For a club in the eighth tier of English football, it is astonishing to see their 136,000 Facebook followers, until you drill down to see that 95 per cent of them are based in Brazil and there can't be many other clubs below the Premier League hermetically-sealed universe that have a dedicated Portuguese section on their website, an elegant language that even makes, 'the Arena is situated off the A3, not far from the Tolworth roundabout' sound romantic.

'A Arena está situada na saída da A3, não muito longe da rotatória de Tolworth.'

Corinthian Casuals, driven by an incredibly astute marketing decision of consistently touring the globe to share its values, took their first bold steps in 1884 by exploring the North and three years later set sail for South Africa. Those values included the achingly quixotic decision in the early days of refusing to take any penalty awarded to them and, if one was given against them, how they refused to defend it on the grounds that, as Goldblatt describes it, 'the foul must have been sufficiently serious in the first place to merit a goal'.

They have visited Brazil regularly: adventures that included the outbreak of World War One, playing Fluminense and the Brazil national side that the English team beat 5:1. The 1988–89 tour stands out with the true values-driven legend Socrates playing for both sides, trotting to the side of the pitch to receive the chocolate and pink number eight before playing 17 minutes for Tolworth's finest. The shirt's power was echoed in another game between Mother and Son in 2015 when, two minutes before the end of a game predictably dominated by the Brazilians, the referee halted play for Corinthian legendary midfielder Danilo to swap shirts with Casuals' striker Jamie Byatt so both players could change sides for the game's dying embers to recall Socrates' spine-tingling gesture two decades earlier. But the shirts had an even more tangible power to do good, as explained by the Mother Club's player/press officer Chris Watney who shared with ESPN (surely a sentence he never thought he'd read) how:

'We expected the highlight to be the match, and in a way it was, but we also had a chance to touch lives in a way we didn't expect. We visited a cancer hospital, and found out that one of our shirts, signed by players from the team and from Corinthians, had been auctioned off and had helped to save a child's life.'

These are memories that simply can't be bought and sold. They even have the biggest behemoth of them all trotting out in the white that was allegedly chosen in homage to Tolworth's finest after two of Los Blancos' founders watched a match at the Kennington Oval. Real Madrid share the colours but represent values through its leader Slugworth Peres both Corinthians have fought to distance themselves from for almost a century and a half. This included, as Goldblatt described, *Time do Povo* (The People's Team) turning their backs on corporate shirt sponsorship to make space for their message:

'Then with just Corinthian Democracy emblazoned on their shirts they won the 1982 São Paulo state championship; and they won it in style. Speaking at the time, Socrates remarked, "I'm struggling for freedom, for respect for human beings, for equality, for ample and unrestricted discussions, for a professional democratization of unforeseen limits, and all of this as a soccer player, preserving the ludic, and the joyous and pleasurable nature of this activity."'

While Corinthians Casuals continued to play in an, eh, interesting chocolate and pink half/half kit for the 2023/24 season which gives a nod to their early connections to the colours of Westminster and Charterhouse schools, their namesake used the decade since beating Chelsea in the Club World Cup to create a stunning third kit and goalkeeper design. But, remarkably, two years earlier, the Brazilian club chose to honour the Casuals by wearing the same colour palette for their third kit as a homage to their 'brothers in football'. When asked, Casuals' press officer and programme editor Stuart Tree summed up the astonishment of everyone connected to the English club:

'It's mad to think that a little club that plays off the slip road of the Kingston bypass in Tolworth has been recognised via a kit from the two-time FIFA world champions.'

Nike went all in on the club connections that included an 'extended lifestyle collection' (nor me). For the 2020 shirt, a brown base with light blue detailing is dominated by a light blue cross evoking Saint George that divides the pattern into four sections. The shirt also showcases a club crest from the two decades starting in 1919. Inside, the Latin legend on the English Corinthians' crest 'e duobus unum' ('the best of two in one') speaks to their shared values underscored by names and numbers on the Brazilian shirt backs using the same shade of pink made famous on the original Casuals shirt.

For 2022/23, the Brazilians created two of their finest designs over a long history of often choosing black to stylish effect. I also really love the purple 1916 away kit with a formal collar and elegant lacing that drives a polo shirt feel with just the right colour tone to create class over crass (I'm looking at you, Manchester United 2022/23 third kit). For the World Club Cup celebrations, the lucky goalkeeper wore one of the black designs energised by details that spoke to the tournament being held in Japan. Inspired by dragons and using the template to celebrate Cássio Ramos, a keeper who has been between the sticks over 600 times already and, despite three games for PSV and a short spell at Sparta Rotterdam, has been a one-club legend. Ramos was the defiant hero of that victory over Chelsea on 16 December 2012. His number 12 is entwined by two golden dragons (2012 was the year of the dragon for the Chinese zodiac).

For the Chinese, the dragon (that has only been celebrated twice this century) represents courage, tenacity, and intelligence and in Japanese culture speaks to power, strength, protection and wisdom. These traits structured the keeper's career. Called 'Gigante Cássio', as well as the classic black, the shirts were also designed in blue, orange and yellow but the black shirt oozes elegance, topped off by the autograph of the man himself in gold lettering between the outsized Corinthians crest and Nike logo that harked back to another classic black design in their stunning 2018 third kit that paid homage to Formula 1 legend and Corinthians fan Ayrton Senna. His gold autograph on a black background sits in a similar position to that of Cássio's and reflects the much-missed driving legend's Lotus car livery of black and gold.

The outfield players of the 2022/23 season also celebrated the Japanese theme as manufacturers Nike drew on the country's deep well of culture. Perhaps rather busy with a flurry of Japanese characters spelling out 'this is Corinthians', the third kit uses an off-white base to pleasing effect in evoking a nostalgic response to the classic Japanese characters. The back collar is satisfyingly topped by the iconic Japanese flag.

Corinthians Brazil may have jogged out for the 2022/23 season wearing shirts pockmarked by the acne of Bitcoin, both shoulders blighted by gambling and a total of seven sponsors on the front of the shirt alone, but there is a hope that this partnership is more than a cynical marketing ploy camouflaged under a netting of nostalgia and that, despite being beset by the tidal waves of capitalism, the Brazilian child of idealistic offspring can, as Goldblatt describes, remember what inspired them to wear the colours that, 'cultivated an aura of Olympian indifference to their own brilliance'. But that Olympian indifference has been sorely tested for the Mother Club and it must have been especially galling for Corinthians and Casuals players who shared the ethos of enlightened amateurism to be selected for the 1936 Olympics three years before both clubs merged.

The honour of selection for a global tournament was corrupted by a spectacle hijacked as a PR stunt for the Nazis preparing the ground for World War Two and the Games took place under the nose of the blackhearted Hitler and his goons in Germany. It must have come as a relief for Great Britain (Hitler had specifically requested a GB team rather than an English one for added PR profile) to be knocked out by Poland in the quarter-final. Their defeat also spared the British players from what many feel is the only time Hitler watched a match when Germany took on Norway, also in the quarter-finals.

The four horsemen of the apocalypse were completed by the grotesque sight of Goebbels, Göring and party deputy Rudolf Hess joining their leader to watch their glorious Aryan race fall to defeat, forcing him to scurry away before full time.

For David Yallop in his brilliantly eviscerating book, *How They Stole the Game* the capitalist 'cure' may kill the Corinthian patient:

'What happens on the field of play has merely become far too often the cheats taking physical exercise. Mexico 86 was to give many examples of this, including one that must have sent any who still clung to fragments of the Corinthian ideals in search of the sick bag.'

Let's hope, for all our sakes, the truth lies nearer the Corinthian spirit than the capitalists' avarice.

21

A Fool and Their Money?

TO CELEBRATE the last day of writing this book before it was pinged over to the publishers being the beginning of April, now is surely the time to look at times when football clubs tried to trick their fans into buying joke designs or, for some unfortunate ones, producing a new kit on that day only for everyone to assume they were in on the gag.

'Engagement' is often a code word for poking the online hornets' nest of intercity rivalry hoping to get a

reaction that adds indignant traction to an incendiary story. That seemed to be the key motivation for Bristol City in 2019. At best confused, at worst apoplectic, Robins fans were treated to a blue away kit for the season, the colour of their nemesis Bristol Rovers. Falling back on history to justify their decision when, in the 1909 FA Cup Final, City had played in turquoise, they certainly did their homework in fan-baiting. As the club strung their fan base along, I'm guessing none of their staff took lunch outside the stadium offices until the joke was revealed.

Rovers had also indulged in some April Fools' shenanigans in 2005. They shared how, to help raise money for Cancer Research UK, the club palette of white, blue and yellow would be swapped for a third

kit in pink. Considering the motivation for the change, this was sailing close to the good taste wind but, after fans demanded the club keep to their joke commitment, the shirts – which gave money from each purchase to the Think Pink campaign – turned into a big success, selling more than 500 and raising over £2,000 for Breast Cancer Now.

Rovers might have had a plausible idea behind their original joke but, for Scotland in 2021, it seems astonishing how so many people fell for it. But the strength of the gag was that, even for people not taken in by it, they still petitioned for the shirts to be made. It was announced on that magical date that the home shirt would change from dark blue to a homage to Tunnock's Caramel Wafers with the shorts celebrating their famous tea cakes through silver and red styling. If that wasn't enough, modelled with a cheeky knowing grin by Liverpool's Andy Robertson, the away kit went all in on that mightiest of Scottish beverages – Irn-Bru. Fans flocked to the shirts and, although they were never worn by the national team, the stock of 50,000 sold out in hours and became a much-sought-after treat for collectors.

The Scotland prank was generally received with jovial positivity (a rare treat in our age of online outrage), but pity the poor designer who, when launching a new kit on that fateful day, is assumed to have been playing a prank. In 2022 AC Milan decided to release a limited-edition fourth kit. Looking like someone who had done some painting with a pot half the size they needed, the obvious conclusion was the design amounted to a lame

version of the joke that would soon be revealed to a semi-entertained fan base. Instead, they announced that each shirt would set fans back €100 and the shirts would immediately become as desired as a *Hollyoaks* omnibus. The club's website was furiously reverse-ferreting what our eyes had processed when they heralded Puma's partnership with fashion brand Nemen which seemed as relevant as Vera Clinic, Everton's 'first Official Hair Transplant Partner'. Milan's apparent pride in promoting theirs as the first such collaboration then hoisted themselves with their own petard when highlighting which city this grim creation had been made for.

Confusing noise with substance, there is a distinct baseline of desperation, 'Created for AC Milan, a club synonymous with style, fashion, and innovation, the new collection perfectly embodies these values by merging stylish football designs inspired by off-pitch football fashion culture together with innovative football performance materials.'

But not all decisions made on 1 April are naff or tricky ones. Let's hear from Trowbridge and District Football League club Dilton Marsh Wanderers' chairman and co-manager Steve Wyatt: 'Dilton Marsh Wanderers FC was formed in May 2019 by two best friends who had aspirations to run a grassroots football club together. The club is based in the small village of Dilton Marsh near the town of Westbury, Wiltshire, famous for one of the smallest train station platforms in the UK. Dilton already had a great footballing history. Bristol City's all-time greatest goalscorer, the legend John Atyeo, was born and grew up here. He went on to score 351 goals for City, earning himself six England caps. The village is also the home of Dilton Rovers, a fantastic youth football club ranging from ages four to 13. There hadn't been an adult team in the village for quite a few

years and as the pitch at the playing field is on marshland, setting up a club was never going to be straightforward. However, with a lot of hard work, the club gained affiliation status and joined the Trowbridge and District Amateur Football League playing on Saturday afternoons. Their first two seasons, 2019/20 and 2020/21, were both cut short due to the pandemic; however, 2021 was to become a very special year for the new club.

'The squad had been unable to celebrate their first two years so decided they needed to do something together once lockdown restrictions had eased. A special one-off game at St Mary's Stadium, home of Southampton Football Club, was announced for May 2021 and then with the squad in great spirit, the club management announced an outrageous kit – on 1 April! The shirt was described as hideous by the three people who had seen it before release; this was the perfect response for the April Fools' prank. The initial idea was inspired by Bristol Rovers' 2005 April Fools' Day kit. Their bright pink strip attracted huge interest from Rovers fans, so the club released the shirt the following season.

'Dilton are also known as "The Peacocks" due to a pair of peacocks roaming the village in the 1990s. So, with a quick bit of photoshopping a large peacock head was placed in the background of the shirt and filtered with the mosaic tool! The design had taken less than half an hour to mock up but the management could never have imagined what happened next. From the moment the design was posted on the group chat and the club's social media, it was clear the joke had backfired; people actually loved the kit. All of a sudden there was a demand from followers and football shirt collectors from around the world wanting to buy it!

'"The jokes on you if this is a April fool because this is absolute." Adam Wade (Twitter)

'"This design is no joke!" footballkitbox (Twitter)

'"This kit is one of a kind" The Club HQ (Twitter)

'Dilton gained a fantastic new sponsor, footballkitbox, and immediately signed up for their Project 2020 campaign to revolutionise the kit world and make a positive effect on the environment by using recycled plastic bottles to produce the kits. Hope and Glory Sportswear (the official supplier to Project2020) had launched its own eco-kit range and they were excited to see the design and more than happy to help.

'The multi-coloured mosaic peacock was completely redrawn by the amazingly talented graphic designer,

Cherise Brooker, and the artwork alone is fantastic! Cherise's autograph can be found on the bottom right of the shirt among the patterned shapes. The bold, vibrant image is set off by the black trim with white cuffs. As a Kick It Out equality chartered club, Dilton advertised the Kick It Out logo on the left sleeve to support the campaign of tackling racism and discrimination in the game. On the other sleeve is the digital autograph of the legendary John Atyeo with the quote "Aspire to Greatness" underneath. Atyeo won six England caps from 1955 to 1957, scoring five goals for his country, including the goal that enabled England to qualify for the 1958 FIFA World Cup in Sweden. Some of the younger players at the club may not have heard of the Dilton-born footballer. Some of the older players didn't just know of him, they had the pleasure of being taught by Mr Atyeo at Kingdown School in the late 1980s and early 90s after he retired from the game. Sadly, he passed away in 1993. Dilton Marsh Wanderers donated to the commemorative blue plaque which was unveiled at his old house in September 2021 and aim to keep his name alive in the village by inspiring their players to achieve great things on and off the pitch.

'The back of the shirt has footballkitbox across the shoulders with Project 2020 at the bottom. The squad numbers were heavily influenced by the iconic Adidas 3D font from the 1990 and 1994 World Cups. Each number was redrawn with a small Dilton badge at the bottom and made as big as possible to really stand out. Italia 90 was the first World Cup that Dilton's management team really remember, and these bold numbers were worn by the likes of world champion Jürgen Klinsmann from West Germany and quarter-finalist Roger Milla from Cameroon.

'With the massive support and help of Hope and Glory, the club have now sold over 100 shirts including sales to the American states of California, North Carolina, South Carolina and Texas, as well as many countries across Europe such as Ireland, Belgium, Spain and France. The kit arrived a week before the big match at St Mary's Stadium as Dilton faced close rivals/friends The Stiffs from the Trowbridge and District League. It was the perfect location to showcase the amazing design and add to the story of this unique kit. On the night, Dilton raised £425 for the Children's Hospice South West Charity with everyone involved having a fantastic night under the Premier League floodlights.

'Dilton Marsh Wanderers have recently released their second bespoke designed kit with Hope and Glory and footballkitbox once again coming on board. But this isn't just any kit; it includes photos of players, friends, family members (including pets) as well as social media followers in a peacock feather-patterned background. The shirt is also an eco-kit as Dilton continues to use sustainable materials to cut down its carbon footprint. The top of the shirt is made up of two shades of pink with a hand-drawn digital peacock design from the manager's recent visit to Plakka forest on the island of Kos, Greece.

'We will wait to see how popular it is but we already have new ideas for next season so watch this space!'

22

The Shirt's the Canvas

FOR THE 2022/23 season, 2. Bundesliga side Nürnberg partnered with the city's Academy of Fine Arts to produce a stunning whiteout kit promoting human rights. First worn for their 2-1 victory against Paderborn on 12 November, one week before the Qatar World Cup began, the timing was an eloquent message from a city famed for its promotion of peace and parity to that bestial festival of intolerance and artifice. Made by their countrymen at Adidas, the white canvas sits behind a simple and stark message, 'Mensch' (human being) written in black. Limited to only 1,000 shirts, despite its steep price point of €99.95, the club's commercial director Niels Rossow was understandably proud of the project, 'As a club from the city of peace and human rights, we see ourselves as having a special responsibility. Right now, we are putting the words "human being" on the chest of the club jersey and are committed to ensuring that human rights are respected in our dealings with one another. On and off the pitch. We are very pleased that we were able to enter into a very

special collaboration with the Academy of Fine Arts Nuremberg for this purpose and that our sponsors made the realisation of the special jersey possible.'

Like an increasing number of clubs, the Germans see their shirts as less billboard and more canvas. Portuguese second-tier club G.D. Chaves also chose to celebrate their connection to art on their 2022/23 away kit. The shirt's yellow base layer is counterpointed by black detailing, but the sleeves share the art, inspired by the late local artist Nadir Afonso. But art is not always taken up for altruistic and community-based reasons. 'Inspiration' at Juventus for their fourth kit designed by Brazilian street artist Eduardo Kobra for the same season had more to do with opportunism than celebration. If these types of collaborations make you think artists can be somewhat self-aggrandising and heady, you can't have read the giddy press release from Adidas that tries to square away the collaboration between an Italian city and an artist based 9,000km away as authentic as a LinkedIn update. Apparently, the geometric patterns on a fourth-choice shirt will 'extend the borders of the sport and build connections with the realm of art to celebrate a more diverse and inclusive world'. To get an artistic perspective, who better to consult than Giorgio Ricci, Juventus's chief revenue officer? He purrs, 'Together with our partner Adidas, we have embraced Eduardo Kobra's visionary mindset with a surprising and colourful kit that celebrates inclusion and excites our audience around the world.'

For clubs like Juventus, artists and their creations are just the next creative well to dip into until all the artistic inspiration has been aped, hollowed out and monetised. Then, when the last drop has been commodified, it's on to the next arena of marketing spin with no reflection on what has been leveraged and left behind.

But not every collaboration is exploitation. Bari of Italy's Serie B went all in on their artist inspiration for 2022/23. In March 2022 they released a partnership

between Kappa and local designer Leo Colacicco that included the home, away, goalkeeper and pre-match jerseys, all designed using the same artistic palette. The octopus theme is certainly out there (especially for the *checks notes* second pre-match design and turquoise goalkeeper shirt) but it is Bari's city emblem, so speaks to local pride and trade. Instead of a sponsor, the shirts display 'La Bari', the previous club name until the 1970s. Contentious as changing a club crest often is, they elegantly pared theirs back to a black and red cockerel's head, giving a nod to their 90s logo.

Sporting Waterloo FC – a beautiful madness

As a middle-aged man, clothes increasingly stand for comfort and function (i.e. they shade away the spare timber with generous fittings). But, occasionally, there are shirts just so mind-bogglingly, gloriously bonkers that sensible sartorial rules and regulations are joyously pitched out and replaced with a freeing feeling of (old) man don't give a f**k. Step forward Sporting Waterloo from Texas.

The club comes across as relatively unremarkable. They don't have any social media other than an Instagram page with 2,000 followers, they have a standard-issue website and were set up to create a community of like-minded players enjoying the beautiful game and making new friends. After being founded in 2010, their mission was to use grassroots football to help improve the mental and physical health of over 150 players who are part of the club as they take part in leagues across Austin.

There are tens of thousands of clubs worldwide set up in the same way, on the same scale and with similar aspirations. But what made Sporting Waterloo gloriously stand out was their decision to turn the design dial right up to 11. Instead of going down the standard route of mixing and matching generic designs from manufacturers working to narrow margins of safety, they decided to throw all their chips on the table and get in touch with one of football's top design houses. Kit and Bone, as you will often read in this book, have the freeing and endlessly creative motto of an outlier

that speaks to their open-source approach to creating the extraordinary.

They also understand their target market. Diplomatically describing their cuts as 'fan first design' they emphasise how 'they are a regular cut, giving a great fit for all body types' (subtext, 'we've got your dad bod covered). They decided to make Sporting Waterloo's home shirt for the 2022/23 season a strident mission statement of how shirts speak to us and, when your club nickname is Medusa, it would be rude not to beat dull to death. Any promotional text from a designer that includes the words 'feature contrasting purple and black snakeskin print' had me at 'purple'.

Where to start on this beautifully bananas design journey? On 5 September 2022, Matt from Kit and

Bone shared some of the steps in this startling design process, 'Sporting Waterloo wanted a unique look for their new season shirt. They had adopted Medusa as an unofficial mascot of the club and wanted her face to be a prominent feature on their purple shirts. I felt we could go really bold with the illustration on this one as there was no sponsor to break up the front. The flat colour illustration style allowed a level of symmetry to the image bringing an easy-on-the-eye balance to the overall design. The design then needed some form of framing and pattern. The illustration alone was never going to work on its own. So a Greek shield motif was added around the figure with added snakeskin pattern to build the design out to the edges of the shirt. The sleeves and back continue the snakeskin theme. The sleeves use our bolt logo stripes to provide extra colour and a natural break for the bold colour change. The back is simpler and features a small symbol that the club wanted to create as a tribute to a former player.'

Honouring former players is a key part of shirt design and club tradition. This was shown by West Bromwich Albion's 2023/24 home kit which paid tribute to club legend Jeff Astle. Astle was a prolific striker for the Baggies between 1964 and 1974, scoring 174 goals. After retiring, he tragically passed away aged 59 in 2002 from a degenerative brain disease caused by repeated head injuries during his playing career. His family founded the Jeff Astle Foundation to campaign for more research into links between sport and brain injuries.

West Brom honoured Astle's legacy by dedicating their new home shirt to him and partnering with his foundation. His daughter Dawn said her family were 'honoured and overwhelmed' by the gesture which continued her father's legacy and raised awareness. Shirts represent club history and icons like Astle are an integral part of that. Dedicating shirts to past players keeps their memory alive while supporting important causes like brain injury research. This shows why honouring former players is key to football shirt design – it respects the past while aiming to shape the future. Now, let's get back to Texas.

Matt continued, 'The final design element is a new badge for the shirt. We continued the snake theme by creating a simple S-shaped snake which has subtle detailing visible on closer inspection.'

That gives us an insight into the design process, but nothing beats taking the beauty out on the open road and logging the looks on faces used to reading tawdry betting sponsors on Friday afternoon phoned in design from uninspired templates leveraging monetisation over inspiration.

Viva this intoxicating insanity and, generic shirtomatons take note. Life is short. Dive into shirts that celebrate a beautiful madness.

Closer to home and more rooted in history over revenue streams, League One club Lincoln City's community shirt used the artistic skills of local designers and Imps fans Gary Hutchinson, Mandi Slater and Danny Nesbitt to celebrate a century of the city's connection to the RAF, their iconic cathedral and the Lincolnshire flag. With only 100 units produced and showcasing the Fans For Diversity logo, the shirt

is also part of a wider movement to promote the bonds between cities and the clubs that sit within them. This My City, My Shirt movement brings together local fans, designers, artists and manufacturers to celebrate meaningful connections over inauthentic new revenue streams for vacuous campaigns. The cause was joined by a range of other clubs including Nottingham Forest, Cardiff City and Bristol Rovers.

Anwar Uddin, Fans for Diversity campaign manager at the Football Supporters' Federation, said, 'What's brilliant about what the fans and Lincoln City FC have done with their #MyCityMyShirt project is the superb extra layer of detail with an official shirt which reflects the club's links to the area and its history, along with the message welcoming everyone. Seeing the shirt next to the iconic locations is first class!' Mandi Slater, one of the shirt designers, shared, 'I've grown up watching Lincoln City. Sincil Bank is like a second home to me and it's a place that always gives me a true sense of belonging. It's the one place I can go and forget about everything else and get completely absorbed in the game.'

The shirt's canvas is then sympathetically leveraged to discuss inclusion and diversity in football's fan base by taking the designs and producing photographic exhibitions across the country for fans to reflect on the threads that bind them or threaten to pull apart. The idea came from photographer Yusuf Ismail and was overseen by Anwar Uddin, as Yusuf reflected, 'I remember telling Anwar about my initial idea and feeling a little hesitant that we could execute what we had in our head, but Anwar gave us the encouragement and support that really fuelled us to jump into the project head first.'

The key driver for Yusuf was to normalise fans of all ethnic heritages wearing the Cardiff City shirts. His exhibition, driven by funding and support from the Football Supporters' Association, focussed on and showcased the diversity already making up the fan base.

These heartfelt, inclusive initiatives create a rose-tinted longing in fans like me. When I saw Barcelona trot out for their *Clásico* against historical foes Real Madrid wearing a logo celebrating Drake's 50 billion Spotify streams in October 2022, the shirt once promoting UNICEF became just another ephemeral marketing influence point. The only people who would warm to the owl logo would be Sheffield Wednesday fans and the shirt, due to tedious copyright complications, was not even available to buy.

But not all shirt fronts are exercises in stilted cross-corporation self-promotion. Once the artistic genie escapes from the bottle, the possibilities are endless, particularly for the rapidly expanding world of concept kit designs. There is something refreshingly free-form and inspiring in watching fans rooted in football give free rein to their artistic impulses rather than worry about bottom lines or return on investments. A perfect example came in May 2022 when one online contributor offered their tribute to Ireland's Bohemian FC which saw a classy design inspired by a perfect pint of the black stuff. The front of shirt sponsor could only be Guinness, the club logo was reimagined using the Guinness colour palette, an understated New Balance logo blended calmly with its background and the whole design spoke to a fan with a plan, empathy for the club and a craft person's eye for detailing.

But the beauty of concept kits is also that we can go, well, bonkers. Consummate concept creator Marci, a Hungarian better known online as Sithuralom, jumped right into the design in late November 2021 for MLS Eastern Conference club Charlotte FC. With Charlotte for its motor racing connections, others opted for chequered flag templates and riffs on NASCAR patterns, but this shirt turbocharged the palette with a set of colours that incorporated the seat patterns of the racing stadium. The nourishing wilderness of colours is structured by a choice to make the concept an Adidas iteration, with the iconic three stripes running across

the top of the arms to provide a calming topping off with the kaleidoscopic energy bubbling up below it. Bonkers, beautiful and brilliant.

The whole concept kit design process has something beautifully off-piste and egalitarian (if you have graphic design skills). For the Loud Kits Design Challenge, every Sunday evening a design theme was offered, ranging from 'fast food' to 'the 90s' and designers had one week to create something stunning before being showcased, reviewed and assessed and a further week for voting to take place. This process described a virtuous circle of inspiration followed by empathetic feedback, leading to renewed inspiration for the next project.

The next natural step from concept kits is the world of fashion. Famously, or infamously, Newport County decided for their 2021/22 season to wear a third shirt inspired by local rappers Goldie Lookin Chain but soon fell foul of the copyright police summoned by fashion house Burberry. Before the shirt was withdrawn, several Newport fans got their hands on it. Rather optimistically, the knuckle-rapped club then wrote to them asking to return their purchases. You won't be surprised to hear that very few of them took them up on the offer. Even more surprising was the lack of due diligence by Hummel. I can only assume the low-profile project was given to someone who didn't know how litigious big business can be when it gets even a whiff of perceived leverage on their intellectual property.

A more successful football fashion fusion came in March 2022 when Sir Paul McCartney's daughter was invited to put her spin on Arsenal's pre-match shirts with her Arsenal x Adidas by Stella McCartney. Choosing to fuse the Arsenal crest with animal print and oversized shapes is the kind of bold move only a fashion designer (or concept kit creator) could countenance but, surprisingly, it seems to work and was generally well-received. Denmark, who made waves with their three Qatar World Cup kits, had previously partnered with a fashion brand and fellow Danes BLS Hafnia. Celebrating a century in business in 2023, Hummel would continue to put their iconic stamp on the kits, topping off the designs worn for a friendly against Serbia on 29 March 2022. Focussing on promoting diversity in Danish society, the shirt designers used a white base layer to underscore a joining together of the logos from them, Hummel and the Dansk Boldspil-Union,

Danish football's governing body. Not only did it aim to showcase unity through diversity, but the match-worn shirts would go on to be auctioned and raise money for Get2 Football Schools that use football in deprived areas to welcome everyone into the Danish footballing family. This would raise a highly welcomed €5,000 for such a great cause. Morten Lund, marketing manager at Hummel, shared the values that, especially through the three Qatar World Cup kits, show why his nation is so admired and respected (are you watching, Qatar?): 'BLS has strong credibility, and at the same time, they represent an unpretentiousness where they are not afraid to do things their way. It creates a strong identity and authenticity, which in many ways is reflected in Hummel's values. For us, togetherness and community are the essence, and in the world of football, there is no "us" and "them". On the pitch, we're all fighting for the same goal, and that's exactly what we want to express with this collaboration.'

Of course, these practical, laudable and respectful collaborations between football and fashion are outliers, not standard-bearers. Step forward Paris Saint-Germain. All the money in the world doesn't mean you have a functioning fashion compass. Not content with making their players dress up as the Chicago Bulls 2006's (admittedly pre-money bags era) away shirt was brought to you courtesy of Nike and Louis Vuitton. Riffing on some kind of smoking jacket/rich uncle's monogrammed pyjamas, three logos of the Eiffel Tower, Fleur-de-Lis and the letters 'PSG' jostle for space in a dark purple wilderness that inspired the club to reach 15th in Ligue 1, half a decade before bottomless Qatari pockets ensured an annual title procession when the next decade saw them have two disastrous seasons where they finished a lowly second.

23

Comfort in Community

KITS AND their collectors have the unique ability to create a close-knit community without the need for external validation, or even to exist in real life. Take, for instance, Kit and Bone's North Pole Premier League, where four teams are currently competing for the coveted title of NPPL champions.

We now go to your match commentator to describe the ice-laced action:

'Excitement crackles through the icy air as legions of fans descend on the Frost Fields for the long-awaited Elf Union vs. Santa's FCFC match. This contest promises to be the pinnacle of the year for the North Pole Premier League. Supporters of all stripes, from pint-sized pixie folk to hulking yetis, proudly sport their allegiance with custom designed shirts by consummate creators Kit and Bone. Elf Union loyalists flutter through the stands bearing jerseys proudly wearingKit and Bone's iconic green and red zig zags. The Santa supporters counter in Force of Fun Football Club scarlet emblazoned with Bone's bold red and sponsorship by Sleigh Navtech.

'Yet the Elf and Santa factions are not alone in their anticipation of the bitter rivalry being renewed on the Frost Fields this morning. Over in the neighbouring section, Rudolph Raiders fans raise a ruckus with air horns and thundersticks, clad in deep purple and sponsored by Antler Haulage. And across the icy pitch, a contingent of Snowman City diehards stand in neat rows, uniformly sporting Bone's powder blue jerseys commemorating Snowman City's tragic 2022 mid-season meltdown alongside the uplifting slogan "Rebuilt and Ready to Chill!".

'As the minutes tick down to kick-off, the energy reaches fever pitch. Chants and songs reverberate as final wagers are placed on which team's superstar midfielder – Elf Union's impish Rainbow Chaser or Santa's FCFC stalwart Sugarplum Passer – will dominate the match. But a hush briefly settles over the Frost Fields as the referee's whistle sounds. The latest instalment in the legendary North Pole Premier League is under way at last! Every frigid seat is filled by rabid fans flaunting their Kit and Bone wares – an electrifying sight heralding the power this humble hobby league has suddenly attained through the visionary talents of two ingenious upstarts.'

Football shirts have a special power to bring people together and foster a sense of community. For fans, wearing their team's colours connects them to fellow supporters around the world – instantly identifying them as part of the same tribe. Exchanging shirts after matches extends an olive branch across rivalries. Collecting classic kits allows fans to wear history, celebrating the heroes and moments that shaped their club.

Beyond fandom, shirts also give people a platform to make statements on issues close to their hearts. When Under Armour created special LGBTQ Pride Month jerseys for DC United, it sent a message that soccer is open and welcoming to all. Similarly, players use custom shirts to highlight racial injustice, support healthcare workers during the pandemic, and spread awareness for countless other causes. Most powerfully, seeing values literally worn on team-mates' sleeves builds connection through shared principles. Captains model

empathy by putting the team above themselves. And organisations like Common Goal unite entire leagues around giving back.

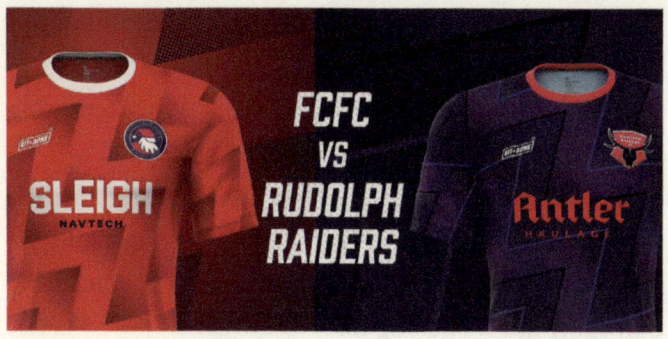

At their best, football shirts bring us together – not despite our differences, but because of them. They turn perfect strangers into fellow fans. Rivals into partners pushing for progress. And messy communities into families, bound by the crest over their hearts. The simple act of fans donning their team's jersey mirrors how shared ideals unite communities. When Stonewall FC players take the pitch in rainbow numbering, they champion LGBTQ acceptance in sports. Yet even less high-profile gestures – a child shyly donning her first jersey, an adult replacing a faded relic from his glory days – forge identity. Life writes loss and heartache on our skin; symbols of belonging ink joy and pride. Boots remember goals scored long ago; a crest over the heart signifies who we are now and who we strive to be.

At times, the stories the shirts tell reveal communities we didn't know we were part of; hearing how her father's 1986 Argentina top connects him to both his homeland and adopted country teaches a daughter what home means, and strangers meeting in a kit swap group discover shared nostalgia in the shirts they exchange – kindling new friendships from memories. Even when fandom fractures, football's shared lexicon gives us common ground to reconcile. As teams rebuild public trust, they'll focus on the values that first drew fans in – because no matter the trophy count, a club is nothing without its people.

Essentially, a football shirt is just polyester stitched together. But infused with stories, it becomes a living history of who we are, who we want to be, and the communities we belong to.